The Pocket Book of
HOME DECORATING

D1589664

The Pocket Book of
HOME DECORATING

Alan Taylor

Evans Brothers Limited London

Published by
Evans Brothers Limited
Montague House
Russell Square, London, WC1B 5BX

Printed in Great Britain by
T & A Constable Limited, Edinburgh

ISBN 0 237 44952 8
PRA 6581

Contents

Introduction
Decorate and save

Written in easy-to-understand language and without pro-
lixity, this book contains more detail than many larger
ones aimed at tradesmen decorators who already know the
essentials.

Read through it quickly; then refer back to pages dealing
with that part of the house you immediately wish to
decorate and study more carefully.

There is no index. Printed indices are all very fine for
quick reference but subjects are rarely under the title that
comes to the reader's mind and he is left milling through
small type leading him nowhere.

So, it is better to make your own index in an address book
with tabbed lettering at the outside edges of pages – A, B, C,
and so on. Then you'll know exactly where to look and
where to find it. *It will also save copious note-taking.*

The use of a ball of putty for removing bristles from wet
paint, for instance. How could that possibly be handled by a
professional indexer? Then again, in the smoothing down
of wallpaper, a printed index would refer to page 104, but
not to the alternative use of a banister brush (page 22).

All products mentioned in this book can be obtained from
good wallpaper and paint shops, or from builders' merchants willing to co-operate, or from artists' sundries
shops. More expensive equipment may be hired from
builders' hire services.

Economics

About four-fifths of a professional decorator's estimate is
absorbed in labour and only one-fifth in materials. Taking a
unit of £1,000, this means that by doing the job yourself
you'll save £800. Saving is as good as earning and this
means that you'll have £800 in your pocket – *tax free*!

If you live in a country other than Britain, translate that

into your currency – dollars, rand, ticals or whatever. Double up on prevailing decorators' wages to allow for overheads – office rent, insurance and so on – and you'll arrive at the approximate amount of a just estimate.

Read first; then act

You'll have to know how to set about the work if you are to avoid the many pitfalls and achieve success.

A source of never-ending surprise is that a new motor-car owner will study books on motor maintenance, yet not bother to get instruction on home decoration. 'Any fool can paint' he may say – and that's why there are so many foolish painting jobs about. That is also why I have to solve over 500 queries a year, not only from members of the public who have got into a mess but from tradesmen who have served apprenticeship and passed exams.

Correspondents range from those who are hardly literate, through the artisan and white-collared classes to nobility. Yes! an enquiry came from a noble duke interested in woodgraining and I had to hare down to the local reference library to find out how I should address him. So if you should have occasion to call on the Lord of the Manor and find a speck of emulsion paint on his coronet, you'll know what he's been up to. But if he has studied this book conscientiously, or got his butler to do it for him, it will be only *one* spot!

Women at work

Women often make better decorators than men because they take more pains over cleaning a surface and in preparation. Chapter 5 deals with this important part of the decorating programme. Mostly, but not always, they have a finer appreciation of colour too. But if I may have the temerity to make an adverse point: Their chief drawback is that when they have finished a room they cannot bear to *waste* material left over – and so use it up on ornaments, coal scuttles and what-not, whereas a man is only too delighted to replace the can lid, put these 'overs' under the stairs and wash his hands. For once, the man is right!

8

Professional v Do-it-yourself work

It may be argued that a tradesman will do the work in a quarter the time taken by you. But will he? He may start and then you won't see him for some days while he's keeping another irate customer happy.

When doing the job yourself you can avoid upsetting the whole menage by working piecemeal. Entirely redecorate one room taking, say, three weekends, touch up another room – one weekend, and attend to one aspect only of the outside which may take three weekends. Seven weekends in all, amounting to only two weeks continual labour a year, won't tire you out or interfere too much with other things. You will also be able to choose your own time when weather conditions are good.

If you live in a detached house, don't think that by working on one facade a year you will show up fading or deepening of colours on the other three sides. By the time curious passers-by in the street have reached the front of your home they'll have forgotten what the near side looks like. And if they take the trouble to turn round after passing and see only the far side they'll have forgotten how the front looks – provided the colour of the new paintwork is something similar to that already on.

With a terrace house you can use entirely different colours at front and back because a visitor will have to pass through before seeing the back-garden side.

Paint v Paint products

Paint is a coating brushed, rollered or sprayed onto a surface to beautify and protect it. What is generally known as a *paint product* relies on its preservative powers by soaking into the surface. The term also covers other sundry items.

Disadvantages of paint are that it is liable to crack under structural movement to which every house is prone. If applied to outside woodwork, rain enters, runs along the grain and, unable to escape quickly under a hot sun, blows blisters which disintegrate the whole film. There are also problems of erosion and 'chalking' of which more anon.

Why then, not always use wood preservatives which, because they leave little or no film, cannot blister or crack? You can, if you don't mind a dull, uninteresting and limited range of colours which are difficult to clean and will leach out by the action of the weather. Some wood preservatives, with which we shall shortly deal, are translucent; that is, they provide a degree of colour, yet show the grain of the wood through. But to be effective they should be used on more expensive timbers than those intended for normal house construction, so increasing capital costs considerably.

Keep this book for reference

By all means browse through books on home decoration at your local library, but it is far better to have one on your bookshelf so that, after reading through, you can refresh your memory by referring to relevant chapters as occasion demands. That is why this one is so reasonably priced -- to put it within reach of everybody.

Another thing: an author draws one royalty only on each book bought by a library in Britain, and 100 people may borrow it before it disintegrates. So spare a thought for the poor sweated writer supplying 100 readers with precious information for only a pittance. (This injustice may be partially rectified shortly.)

Now, dry your eyes and let's be serious!

Alan Taylor

1 Here are the paints

Essentially paint consists of pigment (minute coloured particles), binder which binds these particles together, and thinner or solvent which makes it liquid and easy to apply to a surface. The liquid parts of a paint are also known as the medium or vehicle (that is, the vehicle that carries the pigment in suspension).

After the solvent has evaporated and, in the case of an alkyd resin paint, oxidisation has started, a film is left behind to protect and beautify. All film-forming materials are called paint. And if a leaflet is stuffed through your letterbox by a manufacturer claiming that his new discovery is not a paint he is wrong. In any case it isn't wise to invest in such products. About 80 per cent of their manufacture ceases in a couple of years and then you have no come-back if anything goes wrong.

If he claims that, by using his product, you need never repaint, again he is wrong because the condition of the surface is as important as the quality of the material you use to cover it. Nothing will stick for long over a powdery or loose substratum and, if grease is present, it will mingle with the oil of the paint and result in slow drying. In extreme cases it won't dry at all.

Some paints, such as emulsions, may take over a slightly damp surface but it's safer to make sure the groundwork is dry. With wood, moisture content should be between 12 and 17 per cent which, for all practical purposes, is dry. If it is *too* dry the wood will expand when eventually it rains, pushing off the paint in flakes.

Buying paint

Your safest bet is to buy alkyd resin, emulsion and masonry paints with a well-known name. They aren't cheap; but when one considers their long life the money is well spent.

11

That doesn't exclude smaller reputable manufacturers who, because they cannot compete with the 'big boys' over materials with a large use, confine their activities to smaller items – metallic paints (gold and silver), blackboard paints, hammer finishes, brick, bath and bituminous paints and a miscellany of fringe products.

Paint products

'Paint products' is a term used for a wide variety of materials used in the decorative and protective process, for instance, creosote and proprietary wood preservatives which act by their power to penetrate rather than form a film, helping to kill fungus spores that cause rot in wood. Then there are madison sealers and varnishes, putties, mastic compounds and allied items.

What is known as white spirit in Britain (another paint product and cheap substitute for turpentine) is called turpentine substitute in some other parts of the world where 'white spirit' means a highly inflammable liquid. Make sure you get the right thing!

Classifications of paint

Until recently paints were easy to classify according to their base or medium: oil, water, cellulose and so on. These days, strict division is not simple. To improve their products in a highly competitive market, manufacturers add a little of this and a little of that. In some cases these additives *are* an improvement, making the paints easier under the brush, giving smooth flow and quicker drying, greater hiding power to obliterate whatever colour is underneath, and greater elasticity. In other cases they are, alas, just advertising gimmicks.

Alkyd resin paints

The older oil paints were oleoresinous or based on vegetable oils. In the '30s I.C.I. introduced the first alkyd resin oil paint to Britain from America and called it Dulux.

Natural ingredients tend to vary from batch to batch whereas these alkyds are man-made and, being consistent in every can you buy, are more dependable. After the first teething troubles, alkyd resins became the most popular amongst tradesmen for all wood and ironwork, inside and out. In high-gloss form they give a bright, easy-to-clean surface; and if you object to a high gloss they are also available in eggshell, which imparts a delicate sheen, and matt which has no lustre at all. These last two should be confined to interiors only; they won't stand up to weather.

Other manufacturers were quick to analyse and copy and now most paints sold for house decoration are based on alkyd resin.

Lead paints

For all practical purposes, paints that have more than a minimal amount of lead in them are OUT because of the hazard to health. By British law, those having a lot of lead must state so clearly on the can label.

In the case of children's toys, cots and prams, anything more than the smallest amount of lead isn't allowed in advanced countries. There are other harmful ingredients in paint, but in such minute quantities that they can't be classed as dangerous. All the same, it is safest to cover cot rails with a non-tearable cloth on which youngsters can exercise their teeth. No telling in the world will teach them not to bite!

One-coat paints

So-called one-coat, jelly or thixotropic paints combine the properties of undercoat and finishing coat. They give a thicker film than the finishing coat of the multi-coat process consisting of separate primer, undercoat and finishing coat and, having the consistency of tomato sauce before the bottle is shaken, don't readily run or sag. However, they often require two coats to hide a colour underneath effectively.

These materials are excellent for a quick job and look quite good. But compare them side by side with the multi-coat process and you'll see the difference.

Other one-coat paints comprise the functions of primer and undercoating.

Water-based paints

Paints that *may* have a little oil in them but are thinned with water include distempers, water paints and emulsions or latex paints.

The last named revolutionised wall decoration in the late '30s. Most of them give a matt surface, are easy to brush or roller on, are quick in drying so that a room of normal size can be given two coats in one day – and can be scrubbed when dirty. This is dealt with in chapter 5.

Some modern emulsions give an attractive sheen and they are continually being improved.

Before rollering paint on the main part of a wall, attend to corners and the top and bottom adjoining ceiling and skirting (baseboard) with a smallish brush and following a stippling motion.

Acrylic or vinyl? A question often asked by newcomers to painting! They're the most widely used resins in emulsions.

Without going into technical details, an acrylic is a member of the same family as Perspex, and a vinyl comes within the same category as some floor tiles, imitation leathers and a few wall coverings. There's no need to bother about which is the better. Leave that decision to a manufacturer of repute.

Distempers A true distemper, commonly known as whitewash (not limewash which is in a class of its own) is size-bound and cannot be cleaned by washing. Nothing will take over it without blistering – not even another coat of the same material.

Water paint This is different from distemper. It *can* be washed gently, repainted or papered over, like emulsion, but is not quite as good.

You can check whether a surface has been distempered, emulsioned or water-painted by wrapping a damp cloth over the index finger and rubbing hard. If colour comes off on the cloth it is indeed distemper.

Remove the lot by scraping, aided by warm water to which a little ammonia has been added (to soften the glue content). Then, to make sure the surface is firm, apply a penetrating primer (page 37).

Emulsion and water paints Emulsions have largely taken over from water paints (which are half-way between emulsions and distempers and often erroneously called 'washable distempers' on account of their harder wearing properties).

When rollering or brushing on, wield the roller or brush in criss-cross fashion, but always lay off with perpendicular strokes. Professionals often neglect to do that; but with large modern picture windows, light strikes onto the wall almost horizontally. When laying-off strokes go in the same direction, light will be reflected evenly. If criss-cross, reflection will be haphazard and 'sheeriness' (patchiness) may show up.

Texture paint Obtainable in paste or powder form to be mixed with water. This product gives a relief pattern, using brush, trowel or roller covered with polyurethane sheeting. Excellent for hiding cracked or uneven walls and ceilings. On walls it is prone to collect dust which can be removed only with a soft brush or vacuum cleaner.

Some are water-miscible so that, if you eventually get fed up with them and wish to return to a plain wall, they can be removed, with a lot of effort. Others dry hard and need chipping which would be an almost impossible job as the substratum might become chipped as well. With the latter type, restoration is best done by levelling up to the greatest heights of the relief with a skim coating of plaster. For this reason, it's best to think twice – more than twice – before deciding on this form of decoration.

Manufacturers give full directions for achieving different effects – stipple, whorls and woodgrain. Some are self-coloured and others need emulsion painting.

Only with a very large room could you indulge in the relief painting idea described on page 78.

TABLE 1

Decoration suggestions for various parts of a home. They

EXTERIORS	SURFACE	FIRST CHOICE
Walls	Brick	Leave as it is
	Cement rendering (smooth and roughcast)	Smooth masonry paint
	Cement rendering (pebbledash)	Leave as it is
	Stucco	Oleoresinous paint
	Timber-faced	Madison sealer
	Asbestos	Emulsion paint (exterior grade)
Doors, windows etc.	Structural timber	Gloss paint
Gutters	Iron (inside)	Bituminous paint
	Iron (outside)	Gloss paint
	Asbestos (inside)	Bituminous paint
	Asbestos (outside)	Emulsion paint (exterior grade)
Downpipes	Plastic (vinyl)	Leave as it is
	Iron	Gloss paint
	Asbestos	Emulsion paint (exterior grade)

SECOND CHOICE	THIRD CHOICE
Brick dye	Brick and tile paint
Stone-finish masonry paint	Emulsion paint (exterior grade)
Smooth masonry paint	Emulsion paint (exterior grade)
Limewash	Emulsion paint (exterior grade)
Ultra-violet ray varnish	Proprietary wood preservative
Bituminous paint	Gloss paint over emulsion sealer
—	—
Gloss paint	—
Bituminous paint	—
—	—
Bituminous paint	Gloss paint over emulsion sealer
Finishing coat of gloss paint	—
Bituminous paint	—
Gloss paint over emulsion sealer	Bituminous paint

INTERIORS	SURFACE	FIRST CHOIC
Living-rooms and bedrooms	Walls	Paper
	Ceilings	Emulsion paint
	Woodwork	Gloss paint
Hall and stairway	Walls	'Sheen' emulsion paint
	Ceilings	Emulsion paint
	Woodwork	Eggshell paint or 'sheen' emulsion
Kitchen and bathroom where anti-condensation paint may not be needed	Walls	Gloss paint
	Ceilings	Emulsion paint
	Woodwork	Gloss paint
	Furniture	Polyurethane paint

Limewash

Limewash imparts an olde worlde charm to country cottages. On stucco, a favourite exterior rendering of the last century, it is preferable to a proper masonry paint, allowing such a soft material to 'breathe'. You'll have to make it yourself:

Sprinkle one part, by weight, of tallow in small lumps over 20 parts of quicklime. Slake with sufficient water to make a thick paste, stirring all the time. This will heat up of its own accord; so allow to cool and thin with more water to the required consistency, again stirring.

If there's difficulty in getting quicklime, order it specially from a builders' merchant and, if he shows reticence, ask him for the name of a supplier and order it yourself.

SECOND CHOICE	THIRD CHOICE
Emulsion paint	Water paint
Paper	Water paint
Eggshell paint or 'sheen' emulsion	Matt paint
Paper	Water paint
Water paint	Paper
Gloss paint	Matt paint
Emulsion paint	Vinyl or washable wallpaper
Eggshell paint	Gloss paint
Eggshell paint	'Sheen' emulsion
Gloss paint	'Sheen' emulsion (see page 14)

Tallow is sometimes hard to get; so substitute linseed or castor oil – 1 part by volume to 24 parts of limewash.

A more powdery recipe is 1 part of alum, 20 parts of powdered glue and 300 parts of lime by weight.

To achieve a pure white, add a little lime-resisting blue (ochre for yellow). Add the pigment before slaking and mix well.

Apply limewash with a grass brush or one of pure nylon and with random strokes. The latter lasts longer over a rough surface and the filaments won't get 'sloppy' as is the case with a bristle brush. In any case it is inadvisable to use bristle, which is harmed by lime.

Cellulose paints

These are too fast drying for general household use. They

can be sprayed on motor-car bodies and brushed on small items such as ornaments. See page 81.

Polyurethane paints

True polyurethanes come in two packs. They leave an extremely hard film and so are not for general house decoration where there is always a certain amount of structural movement leading to premature cracking. They also present application difficulties and are wasteful – as the two packs have to be mixed immediately before use and what is left over thrown away. For these reasons they are suitable only for industrial purposes.

Artful paint chemists have, however, evolved a modified polyurethane which comes in *one* can. This is useful for painting chairs and kitchen units where wear is more than usually excessive. If it contains a large amount of polyurethane it isn't of much use outside because of its liability to chip, and some allow water to penetrate at the edges.

Bituminous paints

The fault of paints based on bitumen is that they soon lose their gloss and tend to 'craze' under a hot sun. On the other hand, being one of the most waterproof materials known, they are ideal for parts that require more than usual protection and aren't readily seen: roofs of asbestos sheds, for instance, and here you can get them in colours – venetian red, brown and a dull green. They are also just the thing for the insides of rainwater gutters which are dealt with in more detail in chapter 9.

Varnishes

Old-fashioned vegetable oil paints required varnish as a last coat. Modern alkyd resin paints do not as they contain their own varnish.

Applied to *raw* wood, however, varnish shows up the grain to advantage though it slightly alters its colour. Ordinary wood varnish can be used on interior work and, if several coats are being applied, alternate gloss and matt ending up with whatever finish you want – gloss or matt.

This is of no use outside because even the superior grades used on yachts last only about 12 months. What is wanted here is an ultra-violet resisting varnish.

Varnish contains no pigment to obstruct the disruptive action of the sun's rays and that is why the u.v. type is needed for exteriors. It should last at least five years.

Wood preservatives

Creosote is good enough for garden fences which are more or less hidden by flowers in front. It soaks in only about a millimetre (fraction of an inch) and so doesn't give internal protection against fungus attack. Apply with a bristle brush or garden sprayer – not a nylon brush which will disintegrate with the acid content.

If you live in a country district where risks of obnoxious odours and conflagration are minimal you can, to a degree, impregnate the stumps of fence posts yourself by a hot and cold process. Stand the posts in a large drum and pour in the creosote. Heat up; and air in the pores and cells of the timber will come out. Leave to cool and the resulting vacuum will suck in the preservative. Heat up again and cool several times. Carbon deposit left by charring timber over a fire also acts as a preservative.

Proprietary wood preservatives, which are more expensive, are *claimed* to penetrate deeper without heat and not to contain acid – though what harm a little acid would do is questionable. Their more certain advantage is that they may be bought in colours which, though not too bright, are sufficiently translucent to allow the grain to show through. They are admirable for the walls of wooden garden sheds.

Experiments are being carried out to make a preservative to attack fungal growths and at the same time impart a gloss. At the moment of writing they aren't too successful.

Odour

There is no such thing as a completely odourless paint, though those containing little or no oil are less objectionable. In any case, the smell vanishes once the solvents evaporate.

2 Here are the tools

Fig. 1 shows the most commonly used tools.

The orthodox paint brush can be bought with filling (bristles) in various widths from the smallest to those too large for the amateur to handle unless he has a particularly strong wrist. There are special brushes for varnish with a tapered end to give a fine finish, though an ordinary brush will give almost the same results.

The wall brush, too, can be a large orthodox brush. Distemper brushes are misnamed for they can be used with all water paints not merely distemper which, as you'll remember in chapter 1, has been denigrated as being too troublesome to apply and maintain.

The jamb brush is for dusting down immediately before painting.

A cutting-in tool is for painting up to a fine edge. For drawing paint lines on a wall, a dado for instance, there is the lining tool. You'll need a very steady hand for this unless you use a metal straight edge or can stick on masking tape. The fitch is for fine work and for getting into corners.

The intricacies of a pillar-type radiator present a problem and that is why the radiator brush has been devised. The same curved end is seen in the striker or spout brush, which has a long handle for getting at otherwise inaccessible parts from a ladder; for instance, reaching the apex of a garden shed roof which is not strong enough to bear your weight.

A paperhanger's smoothing brush is designed for smoothing down pasted wall coverings once they have been roughly hung. A clean soft banister brush will do equally well.

It's unlikely you'll want to apply tar, but the tar brush can be employed for creosote or any viscous material. An

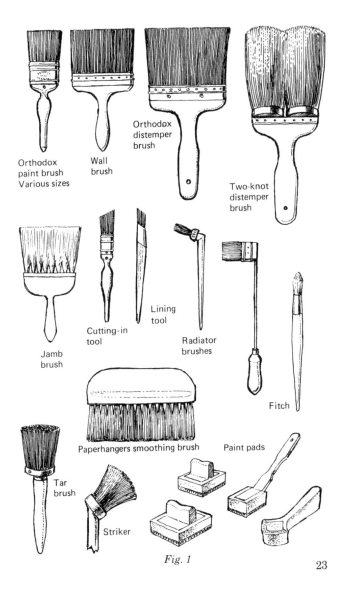

Orthodox
paint brush
Various sizes

Wall
brush

Orthodox
distemper
brush

Two-knot
distemper
brush

Jamb
brush

Cutting-in
tool

Lining
tool

Radiator
brushes

Fitch

Paperhangers smoothing brush

Paint pads

Tar
brush

Striker

Fig. 1

23

old paint brush can take its place; but keep it for that work only, as it's difficult to get rid of all the preservative when cleaning. Don't use a nylon brush with creosote or its filaments will disintegrate.

Paint pads in various widths and shapes to suit different surfaces give a smooth finish, though they're inclined to leave raised lines of paint at their edges and these may not flow out too well. There is also a wastage through evaporation as the paint has to be poured into a saucer-shaped vessel presenting a wide area exposed to the atmosphere. This also tends to make the tail-end of the paint a bit thick.

New paint brushes don't need soaking in these days of vulcanised setting. Indeed, soaking could lead to expansion and bursting of the ferrule. Just flirt the brush (flick the bristles with the fingers to dislodge dust and loose hairs). This flirting should be carried out before each subsequent use of a brush.

Extras Electric sanders for levelling pitted wooden flooring, and fitted with a bag to trap dust, may be hired from a builders' hire service. Steam strippers may also be hired for obstinate wall coverings and ancient paint coatings that refuse to yield to the usual stripping methods.

Minimum tools to start you off

The beginner need not have all these tools. In any case, he is almost bound to ruin his first set through leaving them too long after use without adequate cleaning. For this reason it is common sense to invest in medium-priced brushes to start with; but make sure they're of a reputable brand, not bought in a bargain basement, or you'll be left with loose hairs on your wet paintwork. If a hair does happen to stick remove it by lightly dabbing with a ball of putty.

Later, when you get more experience and confidence, you can replace your first tools with better ones calculated to give a really first-class job. These are expensive and need all the care you can give them. You can also increase your kit as you get going.

Plug-set brushes Opinions differ as to the advantage of

plug-setting a paint brush. This means a plug of wood is in the centre of the stock (where bristles meet handle) creating a cavity at the roots. The bristles come together at the tips, of course. For larger brushes, this system of setting has some advantage when it comes to cleaning the tool after use. For smaller brushes there's no such advantage.

To start with, buy sizes of brushes approximately 13 or 20 mm wide ($\frac{1}{2}$ to $\frac{3}{4}$ in.); 50 mm (2 in.); 75 mm (3 in.) and 100 mm (4 in.). No exact metric size can be given as they may vary slightly from country to country and, in some parts of the world, painters make their own brushes.

In addition to using the smallest brush for narrow surfaces, mouldings and picture rails and also for cutting in, 'hip bind' it (tie half the length of the bristles with string) to make a more firmly controlled tool for narrow window rails.

The next size up (50 mm/2 in.) will find the most use – panelled doors, window sashes, skirting boards (base boards), gutters and pipes.

The 75 mm (3 in.) brush will do for flush-sheathed doors, emulsioning a wall and pasting wallpaper; and the 100 mm (4 in.) for painting outside cement rendering.

The very best brushes are made of hogs' hair which has a natural taper from the roots up and is slightly serrated to hold more paint, while the tips are flagged to ensure an even flow. To cheapen the cost of medium-priced brushes, manufacturers mingle in horse, badger and weasel hair and also man-made filaments. This may sound alarming, but the mingling is done so craftily that they are quite suitable for the beginner.

Nylon brushes

The first brushes made from nylon were a poor substitute, but nowadays the filaments are cleverly devised to imitate the properties of a good bristle brush. They still don't give the same fine finish however but having a longer life – up to five times that of bristle – they're ideal for use on an abrasive surface such as outside rendering. Another advantage is that, with water paints, the water runs off the filaments and doesn't soak in and make them floppy.

In using with cement paint, frequent dips and squeezings-out in water are needed to keep the material from congealing in the stock. Once set, nothing but a strong acid will shift it – and that will shift the bristles too!

You can, of course, buy disposable brushes for cement paint. These are fairly cheap and can be discarded after use.

Care of brushes

Brushes may be kept overnight by immersing in water up to the ferrule – not beyond or rusting and expansion could develop.

To ensure even immersion for various sizes of brush, bore a hole in the handles equidistant from the tips of the bristles and pass a wire through. The ends of the wire can then rest on the rim of a jar of water. It's the paint that you want to keep soft, not the bristles, so don't squeeze it out; keep loaded. Never stand the bristles on the bottom of a jar or they'll become permanently crippled (bent).

For periods much longer than one night, immerse in raw linseed oil and equal parts of turpentine or substitute.

Rollers

As an alternative to a brush, a roller is excellent for interior walls and ceilings and also for outside renderings and pasting wallpaper. It can be used for almost all types of paint, but not bitumen which is too sticky, nor cellulose which dries too quickly.

One covered with mohair is best for all-round work. If you have difficulty in getting one at a paintshop, go to a builders' merchant. Indeed, a builders' merchant is the place to go for anything not stocked by the usual type of shop.

A roller is supplied with a sloped tray to hold the paint and there's a serrated part near the top of the tray for rollering out surplus. It should be provided with a long-handled attachment for reaching heights.

Keep the roller on the wall surface. Don't allow it to spin in the air or you'll be faced with paint splashes.

A foam-covered roller is the cheapest. It gives the smoothest finish and is used only on smooth surfaces.

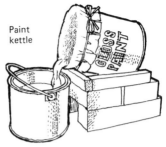

Paint
kettle

Fig. 2   Fig. 3

For textured interiors and outside rendering, there's a lambs' wool roller. This has a longer pile to reach into the intricacies. For roughcast rendering, these tools are sold by builders' merchants which have an extra long pile, up to 30 mm ($1\frac{1}{4}$ in.). It's better not to use a lambs' wool roller with oil paint as bits tend to become deposited on a wet surface.

Good rollers have their covering wound spirally. This gives the effect of a motor-car tyre skidding round a corner and forces the paint in instead of merely laying it on top.

Rollers can be bought in a variety of widths and shapes for getting into corners, and also curved for coating pipes and corrugated surfaces. You needn't worry about these to start with.

When painting outside rendering from a ladder, using the tray provided would present handling difficulties and necessitate frequent running up and down to replenish with paint. You can buy a rectangular container resembling a coal scuttle for this purpose. It bolts onto the stile (upright) of a ladder with wing nuts and has a serrated side.

A good improvisation is a small bucket in which a short plank of wood is inserted for rollering out surplus paint (Fig. 2). Hook it onto a convenient rung with a meat hook and tie its base to one of the stiles so that it doesn't swing.

Rollers are ideal for the quick painting of wire fencing. Roller the paint on one side and, without any more paint, roller out the other. Exudations through the mesh will provide all the paint needed for this side.

Spray guns

With a roller you can work twice as quickly as with a brush, and a spray gun is twice as fast again though, as the paint used will need thinning, at least two applications will be needed to achieve the same film thickness as that of brush or roller application. Then, parts you don't want to paint will have to be masked out with paper and adhesive tape and there'll be a certain amount of wastage through overspray. Outside, spraying can only be carried out in windless weather.

For these reasons, spraying should be considered only on large houses with wide wall expanses.

You'll have to get practical instruction on the use of a gun. It has to be kept on the move at a consistent speed. As the paint tends to fan out, each swath must slightly overlap the preceding one and, at the end of each swath, the trigger is momentarily released to prevent an excess of paint accumulating at these parts. The arm shouldn't move in a natural arc but be held at strict right-angles to the job so that the coating will be of even thickness.

Spray attachments to vacuum cleaners aren't all that satisfactory.

No grit should be in the paint, such as mica particles in a stone-like finish for outside renderings or solid particles in cement paint. These will wear the working parts of the gun. There should be plenty of ventilation in a room being sprayed and, if there's a lot of work to be done, wear a face mask to protect the lungs.

In any case, *priming* a surface should always be done with a brush which will 'tease' the surface and force the paint in, whereas a gun will merely lay it on top.

A spray gun shouldn't be used with creosote or bituminous paint, nor with a woodworm fluid because, in forming a toxic 'envelope' over structural roofing timbers, not sufficient material will be deposited. The usual type of garden insecticide sprayer is the thing for this work – the kind with an adaptable nozzle and a hand pump which needs pumping occasionally to keep up pressure.

Stirring

Proper paint stirrers are made either of metal or boxwood and measure some $400 \times 30 \times 6$ mm ($16 \times 1\frac{1}{4} \times \frac{1}{4}$ in.), with holes bored at the bottom to facilitate the mixing process. You can make your own from any piece of smooth, unsplintered wood. Chamfer the business end for breaking up solid pigment particles that may settle at the bottom of the can. Some proprietary stirrers that work on the principle of an egg whisk aren't all that good because they work in the same plane and don't 'lift' the solid matter from the bottom.

Straining

Manufacturers see to straining before paint leaves the factory. But if you're using 'overs' from a previous job which are bound to be bitty, pour them through an old nylon stocking or tights. General practice is to stretch the strainer loosely over the mouth of the kettle and tie round the rim with string. If time is important, tie the stocking round the mouth of the paint can and prop the latter on blocks of wood. Continue with other jobs and pop back frequently to move the blocks and give increased tilt (Fig. 3).

Sundries

Block sanders can be bought, or use a piece of wood of convenient handling size, say $130 \times 75 \times 50$ mm ($5 \times 3 \times 2$ in.) with glasspaper wrapped round. A refinement would be to stick a thin sheet of rubber on the block, under the abrasive paper, to take up unevenness of surface.

Ladders and portable scaffolding for outside work are dealt with in chapter 10. They may be hired or the cost shared with a trusted neighbour.

You'll need a push-type scraper for taking off blistered and flaking old paint and for removing old wallpaper; and also a draw-type shave hook for getting into mouldings and enrichments (Fig. 4). The head of a screw is often useful for this purpose.

A filling knife for stopping up holes in walls and

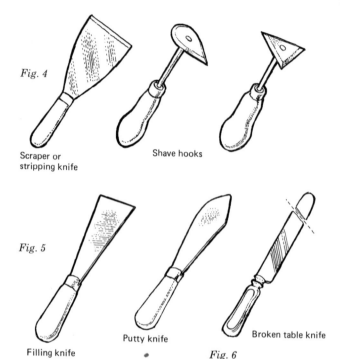

Fig. 4

Scraper or
stripping knife

Shave hooks

Fig. 5

Filling knife

Putty knife

Broken table knife

Fig. 6

woodwork (Fig. 5) is shaped somewhat like a push scraper but has a more flexible blade. Never use this for scraping or the corners will turn up and become worn. Clean immediately after use to prevent rust forming on the blade.

The putty knife is for renewing decayed fillets round window sashes. If you haven't one, use an old table knife with its end broken off at an angle (Fig. 6).

The danger of a wire brush is that it tends to 'polish' a surface and, if the surface isn't too rough, a stiff household brush is often preferable.

Folding wallpaper pasting tables can be stored away comfortably when not in use, or you can use a sturdy kitchen table.

A 5 litre can of paint weighs at least 4.5 kg (10 lb). So always use a kettle (Fig. 3) when working on any sizeable area. It will obviate the necessity of straining a large can should a fly decide to take a suicidal dive. If you are unfortunate enough to kick over the paint (and even professionals have been known to do that!) you will have lost only the amount in the kettle.

Kettles made of galvanized iron or plastic are quite cheap; or you can use a clean used paint can with a handle and aperture slightly wider than the brush you're using.

Old bedsheets and curtains will do in place of painters' dust sheets for the protection of a floor from inadvertent splashes. Start collecting them now. Newspapers pinned together will do for protecting large furniture which may be inconvenient to move out of the room being decorated.

Cleaning up

One charm of water paints and emulsions is ease of cleaning tools after use. They need only rubbing out in water with, perhaps, the aid of a little detergent.

Alkyd resin and all oil paints are a different matter; you must dissolve the residue in a solvent. White spirit (turpentine substitute) is the best and when you have finished you can allow it to settle and decant off for future use. Cheaper paraffin is just as good but, whereas a little spirit left on the bristles won't do any harm, every trace of paraffin should be removed or it may slow up the paint's drying next time the tool is being used.

Chemical brush cleaners (and, if the brush has been neglected, brush restorers) do a quick job, but the writer wouldn't like to trust his *best* brushes to their rather rough mercies.

The orthodox method of cleaning is to press out surplus paint in newspaper and stand the bristles in a jar of white spirit (turpentine substitute) while you clear up your clobber after completing a job. By that time the paint in the stock will have loosened. Squeeze it out and joggle up and down in another jar of spirit, this time massaging the liquid up into the stock. Squeeze out again and rub on a plank of rough wood. Then repeat the dose in a third jar.

Now wash in warm water (not too hot or it might disturb the setting of the bristles) and soapless detergent, teasing the bristles with the fingers. Get rid of all detergent in clear warm water, shake out and leave to dry – but not too near a fire. Hang over a nail, bristles down, in your brush cabinet. Some fussy people (and that's not meant to be derogatory; good painters *should* be fussy!) wrap them in a polythene bag secured at the top with a rubber band to keep dust and moth out. Whether you go to that trouble or not is up to you!

3 When and how to paint

Painting should be done only when there is no frost or fog about and in dry weather, preferably after several days without rain so that entrapped moisture has a chance of evaporating.

Outside Don't start too early in the morning as you'll encounter dew and this is not always readily discernable. For a similar reason, stop work an hour before sunset.

On the other hand, work mustn't be carried out under a hot sun which will lead to premature surface drying. The entrapped solvents, still in a semi-liquid state, will generate gases and cause blistering. Professionals act on the principle of 'follow the sun' – by waiting until the sun has left one aspect of a house and dried off surface moisture, and working on that. When it leaves the next aspect they continue painting on that aspect. And so on.

In the northern hemisphere, climate is so temperamental that, in spite of weather prophets, one is never quite sure whether rain is in the offing or not. The end of August or beginning of September is generally the safest time for outside painting, though most is done in spring to brighten the place up in readiness for summer. In Britain there's more paint sold at Easter time than during the rest of the months added together.

South of the equator, seasons are reversed and in territories having a 'rainy season' – well, wait until some days after the rains have ceased.

Inside Painting inside can be carried out at almost any time. But, as humidity does almost as much damage as rain, don't work when the atmosphere is damp. Besides which, you'll want a good natural light to see what you're doing and to prevent sagging (surplus paint hanging down in 'curtains').

An electric fire will dry out a room. If it is a portable one don't face it against the surface while still wet or you'll get surface drying. An adequately flued gas fire would be all right too. Solid fuel will generate dust unless you light it early in the morning with a good blaze and then don't poke it at all, letting the flames die down of their own accord. Paraffin stoves should not be used because they generate more water vapour than the fuel they consume.

Open windows slightly to ensure ventilation.

How to paint

Dust in paint leads to a 'bitty' paintfilm. So, as you'd do with a salmon can before opening, wipe the lid so that no foreign matter falls in when the lid is removed.

Then stir with a *lifting* motion of the stirrer to achieve a homogeneous mixture. Paint isn't a solution but a suspension of its various constituents, the heavier ones falling to the bottom of the can. The division is not always noticeable, but when paint has been in stock for a long time, the pigment settles and this will need digging into with the stirrer to loosen it.

Paints that don't need stirring are jelly one-coats where you'll destroy their thixotrophy, and also varnish which is bound to have a little sediment at the bottom. If you drag this up you'll get a 'bitty' film.

Now pour a little of the stirred paint into a kettle (Fig. 3, page 27) to a depth of about 50 mm (2 in.) and certainly not more than half full – according to the area of the surface being painted at one time. Replace the can lid and stand it in a corner of the room where it'll be safe.

Dip the brush in the kettle to some two-thirds of the bristle's length and tap out surplus from both sides of the brush, on the sides of the kettle. Don't drag the bristles over the edge or you'll remove too much.

Apply the loaded brush to a top corner and, with broad strokes, *lay on* the paint. Then *brush out* at right angles to achieve a film of uniform thickness. Finally *lay off* in the first direction, lightly, with the tips of the bristles held at an acute angle to achieve a smooth finish.

Brushing out is particularly important and should be

done until the bristles glide evenly. If they slip on one part and stick on another, brush out still more. If you don't, a variety of thicknesses will result in internal stresses which decrease the life of the job. Again, the protective power of a paint depends on its thinnest portions, not its thickest.

Some paints don't need brushing out; and directions to this effect will be given on the can label: cellulose types, for instance, which dry quickly.

The last brush-out should always be done into the previously applied swath, allowing the tips of the bristles to leave the surface acutely – like an aircraft taking off.

When emulsioning a wall, the greatest height one person can manage without a 'hard edge' forming is about 2.5 m (8 ft). Anything much higher than this will need two people.

With a multi-coat paint, consisting of primer, undercoat and one or two finishing coats, this procedure of laying on, brushing out and laying off should be carried out with all coats.

Indoor procedure

Remove light furniture into another room. Heavy pieces can be stacked near the centre, preferably longways so that the ceiling may be reached without too much leaning over. Protect these pieces with sheet polythene or newspapers pinned together.

Carpets need taking up. Remove tacks with a claw hammer or, if there are spiked grips, push the edge of the carpet towards the wall to release it and pull up.

Turn in any recess folds there may be to form a rectangle. Then fold from corner to opposite corner; then the newly formed corners to opposite corners and so on until you get a neat stack in the centre of the room. In this way, after completing decoration, it will be easier to unfold back into position than if you roll it (Fig. 7). Protect with polythene sheeting.

Lay dust sheets on the floor. Granted, splashes will be hidden by the carpet when replaced but appearance has to be considered when selling your house at a future date.

Deal with the ceiling first, working across the room,

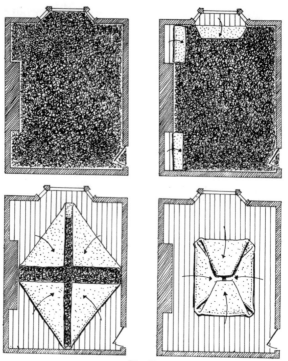

Fig. 7

away from the window and with your back to it so that you can see what you're doing and avoid 'misses'.

Then emulsion the walls. Then paint picture rails, if there are any, and windows. It is easier to *cut in* from smaller areas to larger than the other way round. Now the brush will be well 'worked in' and you can attend to the door. Do the skirting board (base board) last because you're bound to drag out hidden fluff and cobwebs from underneath, and a bit here and there on the board will hardly be seen; though it'll be most noticeable on a door.

If you're using wallpaper instead of any kind of emulsion or water paint, slightly alter this procedure, hanging the paper last. Inadvertent splashes of paste can be wiped off from dried and hardened paintwork whereas it is almost impossible to wipe paint splashes off paper.

Most painted surfaces can be painted over with one undercoat and one finishing coat after sanding down. Two finishing coats will be needed outside to achieve the minimum thickness for weather protection – which is about the same or even thinner than the paper on which this book is printed. You can use a first finishing coat outside *slightly* off colour. Then it will be easier to detect any misses when applying the final coat.

Priming

The welt of a shoe will outlast many resoles. So, a properly applied primer over a clean, firm and dry surface will outlast many successive undercoats and finishing coats.

If it has blistered or become worn or chipped in places, the damage can be touched in with fresh primer after the firm edges have been sanded down to 'feather' them off (Fig. 8).

But where successive coats have built up to an unmanageable thickness you'll have to stop up the damage proud and sand level when dry.

A completely raw surface has to be primed all over, of course.

Wood primer A wood primer is oily, some of the oil being soaked up by the cells and pores of wood to give firm anchorage. For hard woods, thin the primer with 10 per cent white spirit or substitute to aid penetration.

Plaster primer For sealing old plaster walls.

Alkali resisting primer For newly plastered walls where there's a chance of alkali salts being brought forward (coming to the surface).

Penetrating primers These are for doubtful surfaces. But take off as much surface powderiness as you can for their effectiveness is limited.

TABLE 2

Primers

STRUCTURE	MATERIAL	PRIMER
Timber	Structural soft woods	Wood primer
	Porous hard woods	Wood primer thinned with about 10% white spirit
	Highly resinous woods	Aluminium primer sealer
	Teak and other 'greasy' woods	Teak sealer
Metal	Iron and steel	Zinc chromate, red lead, zinc-rich or calcium plumbate primer
	New zinc and new galvanized iron (which has a bright silvery colour)	Calcium plumbate primer
	Weathered zinc and weathered galvanised iron (which has a dull grey colour)	Zinc chromate or more expensive calcium plumbate primer
	Aluminium	Zinc chromate primer
	Brass and lead	No primer
	Copper	Aluminium primer sealer only on parts where a green stain shows. Otherwise no primer or undercoat.

STRUC-TURE	MATERIAL	PRIMER
Plaster	Old	Plaster primer
	New	Alkali resisting primer
	Powdery	Penetrating primer
Building board	Plasterboard	Alkali resisting primer
	Standard hardboard	Hardboard primer, plaster primer, or emulsion paint thinned with an equal quantity of water
	Tempered hardboard	Thinned emulsion paint
	Fire-resistant board	Alkali resisting primer
	Ordinary asbestos sheeting	Alkali resisting primer
	Asbestolux	Thinned emulsion paint

Metal primers Metal primers for iron and steel inhibit corrosion. Note: they only 'inhibit'. If a surface is badly rusted, chip, scrape and wirebrush off most of the oxide and touch in with anti-rustant chemical. Most of these act by turning the iron oxide (which is rust) into iron phosphate which is inert and can be painted over.

Aluminium primer sealers These are formulated in the form of microscopic leaves which overlap like the tiles of a roof or scales of a fish and seal in obstinate stains which might otherwise 'bleed' through the new coating.

Brass and copper Such metals need no primer. Just clean with white spirit and fine wirewool and give two finishing coats.

Lead Don't remove black oxidation. Just clean down and apply finishing coats.

All-purpose primers There are all-purpose primers which are claimed to seal any substratum – wood or metal – but they cannot be expected to function as well as the materials specially formulated for individual surfaces, though they do save time and material. Particular primers for particular surfaces are given in Table 2, page 38.

Undercoat

The undercoat is for filling minor irregularities in a surface, giving 'build' to the system and hiding whatever colour is underneath – though some finishing colours have greater hiding power than undercoats.

Finishing coat

This coat contains the most varnish. It gives far greater protection than either primer or undercoating. It provides the colour you want – either full gloss, eggshell (semi-gloss or sheen) or matt (without any gloss or sheen at all). Use one finishing coat inside, two outside.

Knots

Before priming wood, attend to exposed knots.

Normally, touching over with two applications of shellac knotting will seal in resin which would otherwise bleed through the finished work. The first application can be done with a small fitch (Fig. 1, page 23) covering the area of the knot, or you can wrap a non-fluffy cloth over the index finger and dip into the knotting.

When dry, which will take only a few minutes, make a second application slightly wider in area than that of the knot. This will help to feather off the bump and make it less noticeable under the succeeding paint. But don't carry the knotting too far because paint doesn't stick to it too well. If

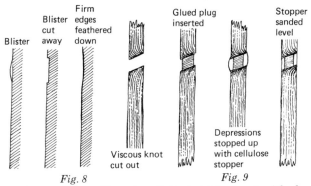

Fig. 8   Fig. 9

you have any trouble, mix a little finishing coat with the primer because this has excellent adhesive powers.

A virulent knot may have to be rubbed with acetone or white spirit and treated with one application of knotting and then one of aluminium primer sealer.

In the case of a knot that is extremely vicious, the only thing to do is cut it out and hammer in a glued plug of wood to come a millimetre or so ($\frac{1}{16}$ in.) below the surface. Then fill the indentation proud with cellulose stopper and sand level when dry (Fig. 9).

Outdoor Procedure

This is dealt with in chapter 9.

Left-overs

Don't throw away surplus paint and wallpaper after a job. If there is a lot of paper, use it for lining drawers. The remainder will come in handy for touching in damaged parts likely to occur when there are boisterous children about.

A friend, one of the highest qualified paint technicians in the country, confesses that he hasn't completely repainted the outside of his house for 10 years. Every year he washes down, scrapes off loose, flaking parts and touches them up.

Eventually, of course, he will have to repaint because erosion will have thinned the film to an extent that it loses its protective value. The action of the sun also causes denudation by loosening surface pigment which dulls the paintfilm.

This *chalking,* as it is called, is a virtue rather than an evil because washing it off brings deposited dirt with it. At the same time it reduces the thickness of the paintfilm.

Storage

Don't place used cans where frost is likely to get at them and make them *livery* and useless. This applies particularly to emulsion.

The best way to store left-overs of paint is to pour them into a jar that can be tightly sealed, so that the paint nearly reaches the top. This will prevent oxygen in the entrapped air from forming a skin.

Another way is to lay a piece of paper, cut to fit the can, on top of the paint – like grandmother used to do when making jam. The skin will stick to the paper and can be removed with it.

If a skin does form, cut round the extreme edges with a sharp knife, lift off and throw away; it's of no earthly use. Then, as 'bits' are bound to have fallen in, stir and strain the paint through a nylon stocking or ladies' tights.

4 When to overpaint and when to strip

With the few exceptions noted in Table 3, existing paint-work can be recoated without stripping off the old – provided it is clean, firm and, if glossy, sanded down to reduce the shine and form an etch.

On oil painted surfaces use waterproof abrasive paper, well wetted, and then wipe off the sludge. But on emulsion it is better to use the abrasive dry or water may drag off the coating. As stated before, new primer need only be applied over parts that have become bared in the sanding process. All you will then need is undercoat and finishing coat all over.

Indeed, a light sanding, wet or dry, is advisable with all old coatings because there are bound to be a few 'nibs' left over from previous painting.

Notes on Table 3

Emulsion will take over old gloss after sanding, but not in a bathroom or kitchen. Here, steam from baths and cooking will penetrate the porous emulsion, condense against the hard, cold surface underneath and the entrapped water, unable to escape quickly, will blow the emulsion off.

Creosote and proprietary wood preservatives won't be of any use over old oil paint because their action relies upon soaking into cells and pores and the paint will act as a barrier.

Some masonry paints are advertised to take over old limewash, but their efficiency is doubtful unless the lime-wash is old and well weathered. Once you have used limewash it is better to stay with it.

On the other hand, we have already seen that *nothing* will take over whitewash, not even another coating of the wash. See page 14.

TABLE 3

Overpaint or strip?

Adjoining text gives whys and wherefores. This list serves merely as a last-minute reminder:

OLD MATERIAL	NEW MATERIAL	DECISION
Oil paint	Oil paint	Yes
	Emulsion	Yes – but not in a steamy atmosphere
	Creosote or proprietary wood preservative	No – because it won't soak in
Emulsion	Emulsion	Yes
	Wallpaper	Yes
	Oil paint	Yes
Limewash	Limewash	Yes
	Other paints	With few exceptions – no.
Whitewash	Whitewash	No
	Other paints or wallpaper	No
Bituminous paint	Oil paint	No – unless a sealer has been applied
	Bituminous paint	Yes
	Emulsion	Yes
Creosote and proprietary wood preservatives	Creosote and proprietary wood preservatives of same colour	Yes

OLD MATERIAL	NEW MATERIAL	DECISION
Creosote	Emulsion	Yes, when well weathered.
Wallpaper	Wallpaper	No. Strip first
	Emulsion	Yes – but not over embossed or deeply coloured patterns
	Oil paint	Inadvisable.

Hard coatings should never be applied over relatively soft coatings.

Soft coatings should never be applied to relatively hard coatings without a thorough sanding down.

Oil paints with strong solvents should not be applied to old coatings likely to 'bleed' through (creosote and bitumen for instance).

Never paint over soft, size-bound distemper (whitewash). It must all be removed.

If a country cottage or old-fashioned stucco has been limewashed, apply limewash again.

Don't use a blow lamp near glass.

After burning off old paint, restore its nature by applying alkyd varnish, thinned.

If you attempt to apply an oil paint directly over creosote or bituminous paint, the solvents in the new coating will activate those in the old and cause bleeding of the colour. After the original coating has become well weathered you can, however, seal it in with emulsion or aluminium primer sealer; but you're not likely to want to do that because bitumen crazes in time and leaves an undulating surface.

You can emulsion paint over an old firmly adhering wallpaper that has become faded through age – but not if the paper has been printed in metallic inks (gold or silver) or deep colours – red or turquoise for instance – when the pattern will 'grin' through. Emulsion doesn't look well over embossed paper.

Oil paint over paper is rather doubtful unless you first apply emulsion as a sealer. The oil in the paint stiffens up the fibres in the paper making them brittle.

A snag about using any type of paint over paper is that, when you eventually wish to remove it, the water used to soften up the paste won't soak through. You'll have to scratch the surface with coarse glasspaper, an old hacksaw blade or the lid of a tin that has had a nail punched through at intervals to form a rough undersurface (Fig. 10). Use all these tools lightly or you'll damage the underlying plaster.

New wallpaper over existing paper – NO! Apart from being insanitary, the old paste will have neared the end of its useful life and the additional weight could pull the whole lot off. You may say: why then use lining paper under a wall covering? The answer is that in this case the paste is new and will have years of life before it.

As emulsion is inimical to too much water, rather than using ordinary size before wallpapering, apply a thin coat of alkyd varnish or any old light-coloured paint that has been well diluted with white spirit. You can actually paper *directly* over emulsion without any sealer but, as its surface is rough, sliding the paper into position presents a difficulty.

As a general principle, never apply a hard coating over one that is relatively soft; it will only craze or crack. Indeed, this is one method of achieving a 'crackle' finish, much admired on old furniture. More about this on page 82.

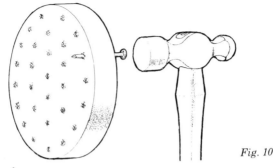

Fig. 10

Stripping

The thicker the coating on exteriors the better the protection.

When put under an electron microscope, flakes of paint taken from 200 years old houses have revealed as many as 60 coats and some old country cottages will have considerably more.

This is all very fine; but eventually the surface will become bumpy. When this happens, or the original paint is very badly blistered and flaking, there is nothing else but to strip the lot off.

A blow lamp is the quickest tool to remove an old paint-film but don't use it on plaster or cracking may result through dehydration. Keep the flame well away from window glass in case you break it.

The old-fashioned paraffin (kerosene) operated lamp is cheapest to buy and run, but you'd be well advised to invest in a more expensive modern gas-filled lamp which is lighter in weight, needs less cleaning and no pumping. The flame is easier to control and less affected by breezes when used outside.

Hold the scraper at an angle under the flame to prevent hot paint from falling on your hand and have a bucket underneath to catch it. Don't play the flame on the scraper blade or you'll ruin its temper. Where there's a moulding on, say, a door case, attend to this before flat surfaces, or the former may become scorched.

Electric scrapers aren't so popular as they used to be on account of their slower action.

Heat de-natures wood but its life can be restored with a thin coat of alkyd varnish.

Iron and steel don't respond to a blow lamp so well as wood. They are such good conductors that heat tends to disperse before it has time to act on the film.

Use a chemical paint stripper anywhere near glass; and if the paint is exceptionally thick and hard, several applications of the stripper may be needed.

Even experts scorch wood when burning off – which means that the surface will have to be repainted, not just varnished. A pleasing effect may, however, be obtained by coating the surface with linseed oil and setting it alight with a blow lamp. Scorch marks are then light in colour and, grinning through varnish, look quite classy. Experiment first on an off-cut to see if it pleases you.

Paint strippers

Caustic paint strippers are effective, but the chemical will soak into the substratum to leach out under a new paintfilm and make it spongy. A non-caustic paint stripper, which is more expensive and therefore only usable on small areas such as those of doors and windows, is much safer. Protect hands and eyes and see that there's plenty of ventilation.

Sand down with fine glasspaper after removing old paint, rubbing in the direction of the grain.

5 Preparation

Like a successful novel that starts off with a riveting murder and devotes the remainder of the book to what caused it, our first four chapters have dealt with the exciting parts – how to paint, tools and equipment.

Now we come to the most important part of the operation and the most arduous, requiring in very bad cases, as much or more time than that devoted to actual painting – preparing the surface.

The vital message in chapter 1 is worth repeating:

If you attempt to paint over a dirty surface, the chemicals in the dirt will mingle with those of the paint and upset its formulation. Grease adds to the oil content and results in slow drying. Moisture vaporises when warm and blows blisters. With a powdery surface, the paint will stick to the powder and down will come painting, powder and all!

So, to ensure that your work will last, see that the surface is clean, firm and dry, otherwise the finest paint in the world won't stick.

Walls You may not be able to get rid of *all* the powder on an extremely friable surface. Do the best you can and bind in the remainder with a penetrating primer which will soak through and render the surface sounder – like a ship at anchor. But an anchor doesn't hold a ship in deep water, and this material is of little use when the powder is thick.

In cleaning a very dirty emulsioned wall with soapless detergent, don't wash down, wash *up*! That is, start at the bottom and work towards the ceiling so that dirty drips won't trickle onto a dry surface causing white streaks. This may not seem important because, it may be argued, the ensuing paintfilm will hide the streaks. But as the trickles run down, the water soaks in, leaving a harmful sediment which can weaken whatever is underneath. By washing from the bottom up, the inevitable droplets will fall on an already wetted surface and disperse.

When it comes to a final wipe down with a wet cloth to get rid of the detergent solution, you can then start from the top and work down.

Don't *swill* an old emulsioned surface as too much water will weaken its bond. This doesn't happen with a glossy oil paint. As a corollary, the grey look of an old emulsion paint is due to its porous nature. Dirty water, or condensation combined with dust, soaks in and, on drying, leaves the dirt embedded in the film.

The microscopic bumps in emulsion interfere with regular light reflection and that's what makes it matt (the opposite of gloss). Oil paint is more or less smooth and light is reflected more evenly, making it glossy.

So, if you *have* to scrub a very dirty emulsioned surface, use the tips of the bristles lightly with a brisk motion to flick the dirt out from the crevices. A worn distemper brush or discarded wall brush is ideal to work with. If you scrub hard, the bristles will bend and skate over the heights, leaving dirt behind in the crevices. Your brush will last longer, too, by brushing lightly. Wield the brush this way and that and round in clockwise and anti-clockwise directions to dislodge obstinate particles.

This cleaning process will bring you face-to-face with surface imperfections which should be stopped up.

Stopping and filling 'Stopping' has, by common use, become synonymous with 'filling', and this confusion has been aggravated by the practice of some manufacturers to call their stoppers fillers.

But stopping actually means dealing with holes and deep crevices, whereas filling means sealing pores and evening out a rough, grainy wood that is still slightly irregular after glasspapering. Filling rarely has to be resorted to, but there's generally quite a bit of stopping to do.

On plaster or plasterboard, wet the hole or crack to reduce porosity and knife in cellulose stopper proud (slightly above the surface) and, when dry, sand level. Don't allow the stopping to spread too far over the

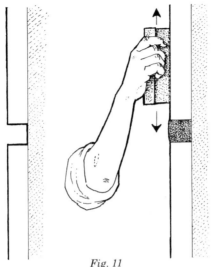

Fig. 11

surroundings or you'll have to do more sanding and, even then, may be left with a bit of a 'bump' (Fig. 11).

Wood Holes in wood don't need wetting as there'll be less water dispersal. When sanding down always rub in the direction of the grain to avoid scratch marks. With a panelled door this means rubbing in different directions according to the direction of the grain of each member (pages 62 and 63).

If, after sanding raw wood such as that of a cheap new door, hairy bits are left sticking out, give a thinned coat of alkyd varnish or thinned wood primer to stiffen them, so that, when dry, they will snap off under further sanding. Then reprime.

Cracks The finest of fine haircracks can be disregarded; paint will hide them. To deal with slightly wider hair-cracks, use a small fitch or artist's number 1 brush to paint in a creamy consistency of stopper, and follow immediately with more stopper, this time of a mustard consistency. The thicker material will follow the thinner into the crack and can be sanded level after it has hardened.

Deep cracks and holes in plaster and cement rendering should be cut back until a firm edge is reached. Then undercut to provide firmer grip (Fig. 29). As stopping shrinks, give two or three applications in a deep crack, allowing each to dry.

Knotting and priming   Dealt with in chapter 3.

Whereas one coat of primer is normally sufficient, very rough surfaces may need two coats so that high parts are adequately covered. This tendency of paint to flow away from raised parts is accentuated where there is a sharp edge. You can get over this snag by drawing a loaded brush over the edge, leave to dry and then prime the whole surface.

Another corollary: When making a home fitment always round off sharp corners with file and glasspaper. One reason for the rounded design of modern motor-cars is to facilitate the factory priming and painting processes.

New walls   Leave new plaster walls six months to dry out before painting, otherwise alkalis in mortar and brickwork will leach forward with the water used in bricklaying, and cause the paint to become soapy and flake off.

This 'efflorescence' shows up as white powdery patches and can be wiped off with a dry cloth, followed by one that is damp. Water shouldn't be used before removing most of the white particles or the alkali salts will be driven back in.

Some plasters need less time before they're ready for painting, and the advice of your builders' merchant should be sought before buying. But don't be deceived by apparent dryness of a surface. Moisture surfaces slowly and evaporates almost immediately. In new buildings there's a lot of moisture in brickwork and this takes about a month for each 25 mm (1 in.) of wall thickness. The period for cavity walls is not halved but reduced to about a third as moist air from the outer wall will penetrate into the cavity.

Even when a new wall is dry it's wise to use an alkali resisting primer rather than the cheaper plaster primer.

You can, of course, give new plaster a temporary form of decoration by applying emulsion or water paint which are porous and, to an extent, alkali resisting. Surfacing damp will then evaporate; but as it sometimes forms craters, these will have to be sanded off before a more permanent form of decoration is applied at a later date.

6 How much paint and wall covering?

Just as mustard left on the sides of dinner plates represents an unearned dividend to condiment manufacturers, so leftovers of paint in tins add to the profits of paint manufacturers – at your cost.

A professional decorator will glance at the outside of a house and the rooms inside and, through experience, will judge straight away how much material will be required. If he errs on the generous side he won't suffer; you'll pay for it.

A beginner without this expertise has to measure more accurately. A *little* over is acceptable for any subsequent touching-up that may be needed. Storing these left-overs is dealt with on page 42.

Average covering power of various paint products will be given on the can label. This will be modified by difference in surface porosity, a very rough surface requiring perhaps 50 per cent more than a smooth one. An outside roughcast may need three times as much as one that is flat. The smaller corrugations of roofing will need one-eighth extra paint than the same flat area, and large corrugations one-sixth. Actually it will take more because raised portions should be given a preliminary coating to counteract the fall of paint into the hollows, through gravity. Then again, the personal element comes into the reckoning. For some unknown reason, and using the same effort, some people apply a thicker coating than others. Whether this has to do with degree of brushing out or the strength of the operator's wrist is doubtful.

A quick way of making a fairly accurate measurement is to reduce everything to an imaginary rectangle, as is shown below:

Rooms   Length plus width of a perfectly rectangular room

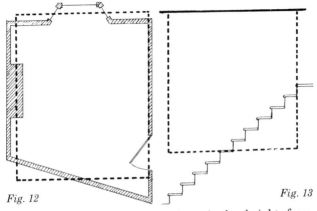

Fig. 12   *Fig. 13*

multiplied by 2 and multiplied again by height from skirting board (base board) to ceiling or frieze gives the total paintable wall area. Subtract area of door, fireplace and windows. Often the area occupied by a fireplace is roughly equal to the height of a wall above and below a window – so you can disregard one or the other.

But rooms are seldom rectangular, so estimate the total by running a length of string around the perimeter and multiply length of string by height of the room. For the ceiling, reduce the surface to an imaginary rectangle as is shown in Fig. 12 and multiply length by width.

When measuring doors and skirtings add extra for mouldings, reliefs and rebates. A typical door will take 0.15 litre (¼ pint) of paint for each side and for each coat.

In your mind's eye iron out the frame, sashes and rails of an ordinary window and the area will be the same as though the whole of the window opening were a flat paintable area. So multiply height of the opening by width and you've got it – pretty nearly, at any rate. A large picture window will, of course, need very little paint.

Stair balusters and also verandah balusters and rails, whether round or square, can be ironed out flat and the imaginary flat surface measured. This could come to half as much again or even double that of the area actually

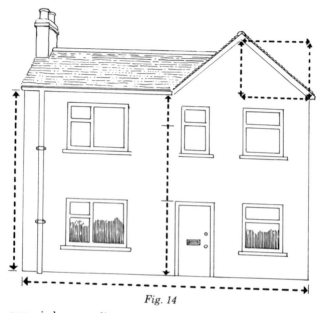

Fig. 14

occupied – according to the width of the various parts and distance between balusters.

Measuring the well wall of a stairwell is shown in Fig. 13.

Outside For the outside of an all-timbered house requiring oil-type paint, varnish of the ultra violet ray type or wood preservative; or a brick house with a rendered surface to be treated with masonry paint, pace along the sides to find linear measurement, not forgetting that a metre takes a slightly longer stride than an imperial yard.

A downpipe attached to a wall will be in sections. Measure one section from stirrup to stirrup and multiply by the number of sections to find the height from ground level to eaves. Multiply this by the number of your paces and subtract areas of doors and windows.

Where there is no handy pipe, get somebody whose height you know to stand close to the wall, stand well back yourself and calculate how many times his height goes into the height from ground level to eaves. Or measure the height of an outside door in a similar way. Add a little more for the edges of overlaps on a timbered house.

In the case of a gable, judge the height from eaves to apex by comparing it with height from ground level to eaves, multiply by the width of the gable, by pacing below, divide by 2 and you have the answer (Fig. 14).

The circumference of a downpipe is about $3\frac{1}{7}$ times its diameter; or you can pass a piece of string round it and multiply by the length of the pipe.

A half-round gutter has the same paintable area as a pipe of the same diameter because there's the inside as well as the outside to consider. If bituminous paint is being used on the inside and an oil paint for the outside, then $3\frac{1}{7}$ times the diameter divided by 2 and multiplied by length is the measurement for the application of each of these materials. Work on the generous side to allow for gutter brackets.

Wall coverings

Wallpaper is sold in widths varying in different parts of the world. Some papers have a selvedge which is a narrow plain margin at each side of the printed pattern.

Where there is a selvedge, trim it off or get the wallpaper shop to do it for you; they have a special tool for the purpose. This trimming must be accurate or patterns won't match and bulges and creases may occur when hanging.

To calculate the number of rolls required for a room, place a trimmed roll horizontally against the wall adjoining the window and make a chalk mark to indicate the width of the paper. Move the roll along to indicate where an adjoining width comes, make another chalk mark, and so on round the room until you come to the other side of the window. Now multiply the number of spaces by the height of the wall and divide by the length of each roll which will be stated on the instructions. Add a little for wastage – say, an extra roll. And if the paper has a 'drop' pattern (page 101), add yet another roll.

Ceilings and friezes to be papered are measured in a similar way.

7 Doors and windows

A visitor awaiting an answer to his ring at the doorbell will have nothing to do but gaze at your front door. When inside and passing from room to room he'll come face-to-face with – a door. Therefore a door should have more care paid to its finish than is given to any other part of the house.

A professional may take a quarter of an hour to apply one coat of paint to one side of a door. You'll probably take half an hour. That's not much time and so you'll have to concentrate on the work. No interruptions from visitors or telephone calls, or you'll get a 'hard edge' to your work!

Preparatory jobs Before starting, see that the door opens and closes properly. If it sticks in one corner, examine the hinge on the opposite side. Screws may have worked loose and will need tightening up. Or the rebate in which the hinge is set isn't deep enough. If so, take off the door and chisel a very small amount of wood away before resetting. Do this gradually by trial and error or you'll take off too much.

If there's a wide gap at one corner, unscrew the hinge and pad it out with a thin sheet of card. Fig. 15 is very much exaggerated for the purpose of illustration.

It is extremely important to check these points before rushing for a plane to shave off sticking parts. Timber swells with moisture and if you go away and leave the house unheated it will shrink when you return and then you'll be left with a gap in place of a tight fitting.

Remove door knobs and finger plates. Leaving them on and 'cutting round' with a brush will take just as long and make your work look amateurish, particularly as you're almost bound to overpaint onto the fitting. The wider the area you have for the sweep of a brush, the better the job will look.

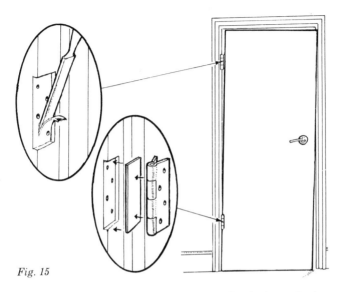

Fig. 15

Flush-sheathed door The sequence of painting a flush-sheathed door (Fig. 16) is similar to that of painting a wall (page 34) except that you work in horizontal swaths. Start at one corner and brush on the paint vertically. Then brush out horizontally. Continue with another band alongside, brushing out towards the previously applied band. Carry on until the other side of the door is reached.

Now brush out again, this time right across to make sure the coating is uniform in thickness. Finally, lay off *downwards* with light strokes.

Start on the second swath underneath in the same way, but this time laying off vertically *upwards* into the first swath, so avoiding a blob of paint in the middle.

Proceed until you reach the bottom of the door, laying off upwards each time. Edges can be dealt with as you go so that a 'fatty' build-up doesn't develop.

Paint the top edge of an old door to make dusting easier. The wood of a new door may be slightly damp, so leave this edge bare for moisture to escape until you repaint at a

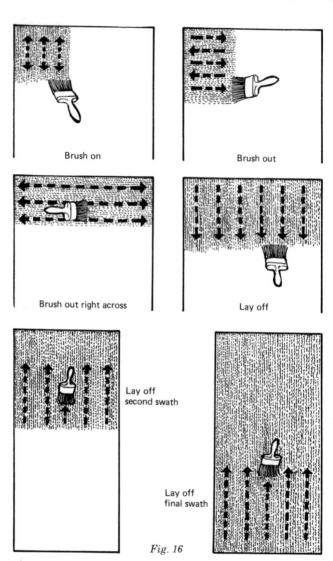

Brush on

Brush out

Brush out right across

Lay off

Lay off
second swath

Lay off
final swath

Fig. 16

future date. Unless it's inconvenient, it's better to leave a new door unhung in the room for a few weeks to reach ambient humidity.

Panelled door A moment's reflection will indicate that the above procedure is of no use with a panelled door. If you attempt to follow it you'll get into a hopeless mess because laying off has to be carried out in different directions according to the way panels, muntins, rails and stiles are constructed.

Most paint manufacturers issue leaflets giving the correct procedure shown in Fig. 17; but they don't say why it should be carried out in this way.

By starting on the doorcase (frame) any inadvertent paint splashes will land on an unpainted surface and can be wiped off.

Next, by doing the panel moulding of one panel you'll get an overlap of paint on the adjoining muntin, rails and stile. So you can take some of this up by working now on the adjoining panel. Carry on in the same way with all panels.

Then attend to the muntins, taking up the overlap on that side of the panel mouldings.

The overlap from the muntins and top and bottom mouldings will be taken up when you do the rails. And last, on painting the stiles you'll take up the last of the panel moulding overlaps.

Look back occasionally to make sure there are no drips at the corners of the mouldings caused by applying too much paint on these parts. Brush them out immediately or they'll start setting and cause 'pick-up'.

When painting a panel you may find that, when starting at the juncture with the moulding, the paint runs thick then thin then thick again. To obviate this fault, apply the brush some 25 mm (1 in.) away from the moulding, glide it towards the moulding and then sweep away towards the centre. Start again at the other side of the panel in the same way, joining up in the middle and allowing the brush to leave the surface at an acute angle.

Brushing out to the extreme edge of a rail or stile is simplified by gliding the brush outwards towards the edges

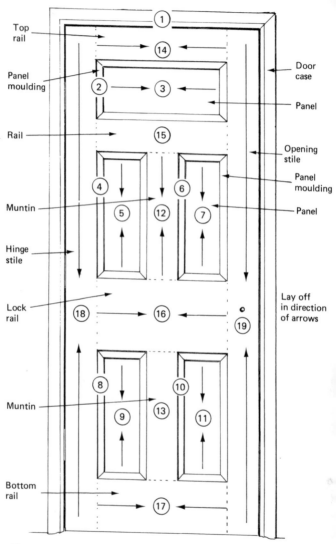

Top rail

Panel moulding

Rail

Muntin

Hinge stile

Lock rail

Muntin

Bottom rail

Door case

Panel

Opening stile

Panel moulding

Panel

Lay off in direction of arrows

62

Fig. 17

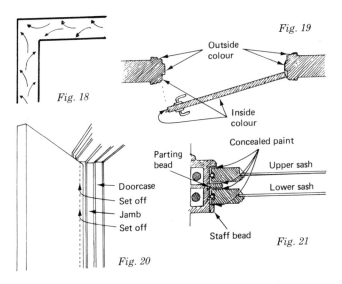

Fig. 18

Fig. 19

Outside colour

Inside colour

Concealed paint

Parting bead

Upper sash

Lower sash

Doorcase

Set off

Jamb

Set off

Staff bead

Fig. 20

Fig. 21

(Fig. 18), afterwards laying off straight in the direction of the grain of the wood.

It's unlikely you'll want to paint both sides of a door at the same time and the question arises as to what colour the edges should be. Open the door half way and whatever parts are visible from the inside use that colour. Leave the other edges until you're painting the outside (Fig. 19).

A fatty accumulation of old paint may have built up on a vertical door jamb leaving set-off lines on the hinge stile of the door (Fig. 20). Scrape this off to prevent future trouble.

Windows

The three main types of window are casement (side-hinged like a door), sliding-sash (two windows sliding up and down) and transom (top hinged and generally found over a casement window). There are also louvre windows that look somewhat like a venetian blind and, because the fittings are generally of aluminium, they don't need painting. Paint might even gum up their works!

A window doesn't need quite such a fine finish as a door. Inside it is partially hidden by curtains and outside it is generally separated from street-gazers by a front garden and so is not subject to the same close inspection. At the same time, it needs care, particularly with preparation because it's one of the most exposed parts of a house.

Remove catches and handles before starting work.

As with a panelled door, paint cross bars and rails that butt onto other members. Then deal with other parts.

We have suggested doing a doorcase first. With a window reverse the procedure because you'll have to use a step-ladder and will want something dry to support yourself.

For edges that can be seen from the inside when the window is open, use the same colour. Leave the remainder until you deal with the outside.

Sticking windows A casement or top-hinged transom window often sticks because of a fatty edge on the meeting stile. Scrape it off with a shave hook or scraper before starting to paint. Another more serious reason is dovetail joints coming adrift through frequent opening and closing. Hammer these gently home with a wooden mallet so that you don't crack the glass, and secure with a countersunk brass screw (let into the wood with a brace and countersink bit; brass to avoid rust). Stop up the depression proud with putty or hard stopping, and sand level when dry.

The sticking of a sliding-sash window is generally caused through old congealed paint accumulating between stiles and corresponding beads (Fig. 21). This means that the sashes have to come out for scraping. There's no difficulty in removing them though it's quite a lengthy job. While you're about it renew the sash cords; they're bound to have had their best days and doing the job after painting messes up your work.

Renewing sash cords Fig. 22: (1) Open the top sash wide and cut the four exposed cords close to the sashes. Use a hacksaw if your knife isn't sharp enough. (2) Prise out staff beads at one side and bottom by inserting a broad blunt

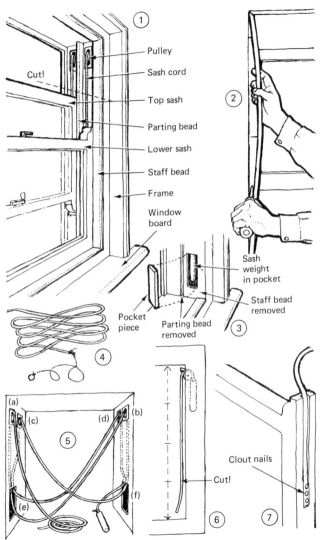

Pulley

Sash cord

Cut!

Top sash

Parting bead

Lower sash

Staff bead

Frame

Window board

Pocket piece

Parting bead removed

Sash weight in pocket

Staff bead removed

Clout nails

Cut!

Fig. 22

chisel in the middle and pull them out. They'll be fastened by three nails; and if the two end nails aren't sufficiently released cut them through with a hacksaw, pulling out the ends with pincers. Lift out the lower sash, remove what is left of the old cord and clean up. (3) Prise out parting beads on each side and the upper sash will come out. Scrape old congealed paint from edges of beads and both sashes. This will reveal the pockets. Prise out the pocket pieces and lift out the lower sash weights. Put your hand in the pockets and push aside a loosely attached dividing lath to reach the upper sash weights. Untie ends of cords attached to weights. (4) Tie one end of a length of stout thread to a 'mouse' (nut or screw or short piece of metal chain small enough to ride over the pulley), and the other end to a hank of new cord (waxed variety will last longest). (5) Insert the mouse over pulley (a) and allow to drop until you can pull it out of pocket (e) drawing the attached cord with it. Insert the mouse over pulley (b) and allow it to drop until you can pull it out of pocket (f). Insert the mouse over pulley (c) and draw through pocket (e). Insert the mouse over pulley (d) and draw through pocket (f). Detach thread from sash cord and tie that end of the cord to a sash weight, making sure that no free ends are hanging loose to interfere with its passage up and down. Return the weight on the farther side of the loose dividing lath. (6) Pull the weight to the top and measure three-quarters down from the top of the window opening. Cut the cord there and exert strength to stretch the cord and firm the knot connecting it to the weight. Drive a soft wood wedge over the pulley to keep it temporarily in position. Tie the end of the uncut cord to another weight and place it in the opposite pocket, again on the farther side of the dividing lath.

Carry on with the other two sash weights, this time keeping them on the near side of the dividing lath. (7) Attach the free end of the cord passing over pulley (d) to the right-hand groove of the upper sash with one clout nail driven in near the end of the groove. Take out the wedge in pulley (d). Attach the cord passing over pulley (c) to the left hand groove of the upper sash with a clout nail. Take out the wedge in pulley (c). Replace the upper sash in position and test that it opens and closes properly. In ninety-nine cases out of a hundred it will. But if yours is the unfortunate hundredth case, you'll have to readjust the clout nails in the grooves of the sash.

Having assured yourself it works as it should, drive in two more clout nails near the first one. These nails *must* be near the ends of the cords and grooves or they will foul the pulleys. Replace the upper sash permanently. Replace the pocket pieces. Replace parting beads.

Carry on with the same procedure with the lower sash whose cords will ride over pulleys (b) and (a), this time placing the sash weights on the near sides of the dividing laths. Replace staff beads and punch in the nail heads below the surface, stopping up depressions with putty.

It seems a complicated job, but it takes longer to describe than to do it.

Never paint a sash cord. Pull it clear with one hand and pass the paint brush underneath, otherwise the fibres will stiffen and snap off when passing over the pulley, so weakening the cord.

Sashes that won't close Sometimes there's a difficulty in snapping fast the catches of a sliding-sash window. This is caused by a fatty edge of old paint that has run down the bottom rail preventing the sash from closing tightly. Scrape off this accumulation.

Rattling of the upper sash can be cured by replacing the parting bead with a thicker one. The same can be done with a rattling lower sash; or, when replacing the staff bead you can nail it slightly nearer the sash. The use of a wedge is to be deprecated and will waste time when you're opening or closing the window.

Modern sash windows operate on a spring principle and so no cords are involved.

Painting the sashes The difficulty of painting a sliding-sash window is that you generally have to stand on a stepladder and hold on to something to keep your balance. So, unlike a door, leave the frame until last. Another difficulty is getting at the top and bottom rails when the

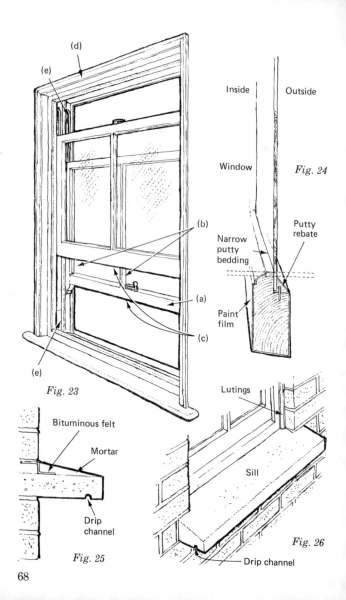

(d)

(e)

(b)

(a)

(c)

(e)

Fig. 23

Inside   Outside

Window   *Fig. 24*

Narrow
putty
bedding

Putty
rebate

Paint
film

Bituminous felt

Mortar

Drip
channel

Fig. 25

Lutings

Sill

Fig. 26

Drip channel

window is closed and gumming yourself up when dealing with the meeting rails with the window open.

See Fig. 23. Working from the inside, pull the top sash down and the bottom sash up to their fullest extent. Paint the top meeting rail (a) and as far up bars and stiles as you can go (b). Then paint the bottom and top edges (c) and the soffit (d), carrying the brush a little down each of the outside pulley runners (e) and rounding off neatly. There's no need to paint the whole of the runner as it is more or less protected from weather. In winter, the window will be closed and in summer it will be open only slightly. And too much paint on these parts may cause side sticking. You can paint the whole of the bottom outside runner.

Reverse the process for the bottom sash. Both sashes should now be nearly but not quite closed so that you can work on the remainder. Give the pulley stiles the thinnest coat possible (in the case of a previously painted window, give them a finishing coat only to obviate the possibility of sticking). Use a dryish brush when painting the beads to avoid future build-up.

Open and close the windows once or twice a day for a week after finishing work to break any bridging film.

Outside

The painting of the outside of all windows follows a similar procedure to that inside. But first examine the putty rebate holding the glass pane. This often pulls away from the glass, cracks or breaks, particularly on the lower rail which gets more than bad treatment through rain running down the glass.

If this is neglected, water will seep through to the wood, lift off the paintfilm or cause rot.

Holding a broken table knife (Fig. 6, page 30) horizontally at the weakest part of the damaged putty, tap it gently with a hammer and the putty will chip off. Glasspaper down the exposed rebate and touch in with wood primer so that too much oil from the new putty won't be absorbed.

Where there is only slight cracking, you can often stop up with Swedish putty which is whiting mixed with paint.

69

Now clean the window. If you don't and a shower of rain descends before your new paint is quite dry, dirty water will become embedded.

Scrape off blobs of paint from the edge of the glass and rub vigorously with methylated spirit. Unless this edge is scrupulously clean, the putty won't stick for any length of time. When the primer in the rebate is dry, 'ball' up a little new putty in the palm. If it's too hard, knead in a very little linseed oil. If too soft for easy working, roll in newspaper to absorb surplus oil. Feed the ball through the fingers into the rebate and finish off at an angle with a putty knife (Fig. 6, page 30). To make a neat job, finish off the putty 4 mm ($\frac{3}{8}$ in.) lower than the inside rebate so that when finishing coats are brought up onto the glass (which will be described in a few minutes) it won't show from the inside (Fig. 24).

New putty should be painted after a week when it will have started to harden, and not more than about six weeks after application or it will be too hard.

When brushing on finishing coats to the sashes, carry onto the glass for about 4 mm ($\frac{3}{8}$ in.) to protect the edge of the putty. If you're steady enough, do this freehand. If not, use a short length of thin zinc or aluminium as a straight edge, moving it along as you go. Don't use masking tape because you'll have to wait until the paint dries before peeling it off and this will leave a 'step' to entrap rain.

Use finishing coats only on the glass as neither primer nor undercoating has the same adhesive properties on such a hard, smooth surface. But don't be too finnicky. A slight overlap here and there won't do any harm.

Metal windows Scrape off rusty patches, rub with emery cloth and touch in with an anti-rustant before painting. Red patches may even then form in time, due to spread of iron oxide from the rebate holding the glass, which is inaccessible. You'll have to put up with this until the pane needs renewing and then scrape and treat with anti-rustant. Indeed, the pane *will* eventually need renewing because iron expands on oxidising and presses against the glass causing it to crack.

Don't use linseed oil putty for the outside fillet of metal windows. A special metal putty is sold for the purpose.

Plastic windows Though it is more stable than wood, PVC has not been popular for doors because of difficulty of repainting in a colour different to that provided. Even if the paint is confined to finishing coats only it will have poor adhesion and can easily be kicked off. Window sashes are safer in this respect; and outside, the integral white shows up well against a different colour on surrounding woodwork.

Sills Stone and concrete outside window sills require little attention apart from painting with the same alkyd resin paint you use on the windows. But if there are signs of efflorescence, apply alkali resisting primer first. Alternatives to alkyd resin paint are masonry paint or outdoor grade emulsion.

If the slope is insufficient to run off rainwater, chip the surface slightly with a cold chisel and hammer, and brush on polyvinyl acetate (PVA adhesive) and add a little PVA to a mortar mix consisting of about 1 part by volume to 4 of fine sand. Trowel on, inserting a narrow strip of bituminous felt to prevent rain that may soak in from reaching the window frame (Fig. 25). Check that the drip channel under the sill is clear of cobwebs and congealed paint.

If the lutings (cement fillets joining frame to surrounding masonry) have cracked or show gaps, rake them out and knife in mastic compound which will 'give' with further structural movement. If this tends to curl at the surface after a few days, knife it back in until it dries. In any case, the under part of the mastic will remain firm (Fig. 26).

Wooden sills are generally of hard wood, such as porous oak. Give these a liberal coat of wood primer thinned with 10 to 15 per cent white spirit so that it will soak in. Then give a normal coat of primer on top and follow with an undercoat and two finishing coats of an alkyd resin paint. Boiled linseed oil can be used as a substitute for thinned wood primer if it is allowed to dry thoroughly before further painting.

71

If you don't do something like this, minute columns of air will be entrapped in the pores and expand under a hot sun to blow bubbles which, on bursting, allow rain to enter, run along with the grain and push the whole lot off.

Oak is ridgy by nature and, if there's not sufficient slope, these ridges will hold water to form small lakes. Scrape the high parts level with a Skarsten scraper.

Some painters use emulsion as a primer with the idea that, as it is porous, moisture will run laterally and escape through a weak point. This practice is questionable, particularly as there may be no weak point for escape.

One certain thing is that however carefully you treat a sill, owing to its tilt vis à vis rain and sun, it'll require attention twice as frequently as other parts of the house.

Sills serving bay windows naturally have to be joined at the corners; and the joins tend to open and close with differing temperatures and degrees of humidity. If they rot at these parts, scrape clean and stop up with hard stopping, securing underneath, if necessary, with a short mild steel bracket.

8 Painting occasional items

To ensure a superfine finish on flat surfaces, such as mantelshelves and dressing-table tops that are readily noticed, make sure your brushes are scrupulously clean and the paint is free from bits. As overhead foot-treads and outside heavy traffic will shake a house sufficiently to dislodge dust from otherwise inaccessible parts to land on your new paint, wait until late at night when children are in bed and lorries safely garaged. Make sure you have a good spotlight on your work.

Sweep and vacuum the floor some hours earlier and, before starting work, sprinkle with water. Apply the paint thinly and lay off with extra care. If the existing paint isn't damaged but just faded, apply one finishing coat only after removing old nibs with flour grade abrasive paper, wiping off and rubbing over with a tack rag (cloth impregnated with a sticky varnish, obtainable at good paintshops).

Primer won't be necessary unless bare wood shows. Don't use undercoat which, being highly pigmented, tends to dry ribbily and the finishing coat will follow these brushmarks faithfully. You can apply undercoat with a foam-covered roller and, when dry, rub down with flour grade glasspaper; but this shouldn't be necessary.

Cigarette burns   There's always the careless visitor (never yourself!) who leaves a cigarette to burn itself out on the edge of furniture.

Scrape out the charred channel with a sharp-pointed knife and fill proud with cellulose stopper brought to the right consistency with a little of the paint you intend using. Sand level when dry following the grain of the wood. Now sand the whole of the surface with flour grade abrasive paper to form a slight etch and reduce gloss. Wipe off and rub with a tack rag. Then apply finishing coat all over.

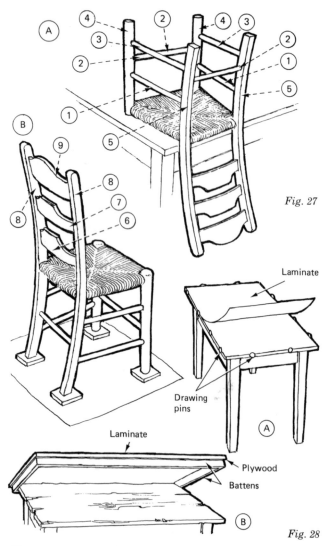

Fig. 27

Laminate

Drawing pins

(A)

Laminate

Plywood

Battens

(B)

Fig. 28

74

Chairs To paint a chair without gumming up your elbows, reverse the usual procedure of working from the top down and, instead, work from the bottom up.

Stand the chair upside-down on a workbench or table and paint in the sequence shown in Fig. 27 (A). By so doing your arms will touch only unpainted woodwork. Now turn it right-side up (B) and, standing it on blocks of wood over newspaper on the floor, finish the back, leaving the top rail until last so that you have something dry to catch hold of. Flick off any drips that may form under the rails with a dryish brush. Note: the rails are done before the legs so that overbrushing onto the legs is taken up when painting the legs.

Kitchen chairs require an extra amount of preparatory cleaning, especially the back top rail which is handled most by greasy hands. Wash off all traces of cleanser you use and leave for overnight drying because moisture will have crept into mortised joints.

Scrub wicker chairs and remove any soapless detergent used with clear water. Leave for overnight drying and apply new paint with a paint pad which will reach the intricacies easier than a brush. Or you can use an aerosol paint, though it's expensive and wasteful of material through overspray. All surroundings have to be masked out or curtained off when spraying.

Tables A table can be painted in a way similar to a chair. Turn it upside-down and attend to the legs. Then turn it right-side up and paint the top.

You can cover the top with laminated sheeting, sticking drawing pins in the sides with edges protruding to act as a cradle into which the sheeting can be dropped in the precise position. Fig. 28 (A).

If the table is old and has an uneven surface make a movable laminated top. You can then remove the top and use the rough table for standing or working on (B).

Butt-join a framework of 12×18 mm ($\frac{1}{2} \times \frac{3}{4}$ in.) for a small table to fit precisely over the edges of the top. Stouter battens will be required for a large table.

Square up and glue and pin on a piece of plywood to hold

the frame rigid and stick the laminated sheeting on top. Hide the join between plywood and battens with edging.

This heightens the table by only a fraction; and if this fraction is too much for your liking, justify by sawing a little off the bottom of the legs.

Radiators A panel radiator is easy to paint. To reach the sides of a pillar-type radiator, use a radiator brush (Fig. 1, page 23).

A new radiator will probably be shop-primed. After installation clean it with white spirit and a coarse cloth. Touch in any scratches with zinc chromate primer and apply to the whole surface two thin finishing coats of either alkyd resin or polyurethane paint. Don't use an undercoat – it won't stand the heat.

The colour you use doesn't affect heat emission to any marked extent, so choose whatever you like. Nor does it matter much whether the finish is glossy or matt, though gloss is easier to clean; and there's a theory that a matt surface tends to hold hot air close to the radiator instead of allowing it to spread out, but this is only a theory and a debatable one at that.

All light colours deepen in time under the influence of heat, particularly those based on oil. For this reason a polyurethane may be preferable to an alkyd resin; though the former does not offer such a wide colour range.

If you wish to use a metallic paint avoid those with coarse metal particles which will float to the surface of a coating forming a thin sheet of metal which, at certain temperatures, can slow down heat emission by at least 15 per cent. Use gold or aluminium paint with finely milled particles so that they remain enveloped in medium when dry. You can ensure the right type by buying a good paint and then by trial and error on any odd piece of metal, testing the surface with the tips of the fingers.

If your radiator has already been painted in a coarsely milled metallic colour, clean with white spirit and apply two thin coats of polyurethane varnish or paint and delay in heat transmission will be reduced. *It is the final coat that counts*!

Refrigerators Scrape off rust and rub with emery cloth. Treat bared steel with an anti-rustant and touch in with polyurethane paint. This will look patchy when dry; so rub the whole surface with fine glasspaper and entirely recoat.

Cookers and washing machines Treat the same as for refrigerators but, with the former, don't go too near intense heat and, with the latter, avoid parts likely to be continually splashed with detergent unless it can be wiped off immediately.

Baths A bath that is merely stained can be restored with one of the many bath stain removers on the market. These chemicals won't avoid 'pitting' caused through hard water.

If a bath needs complete repainting, better than attempting the work yourself, get a professional bath refinisher to do it properly. He will work *in situ* and won't interfere with either plumbing or existing decorations.

You can do a *passable* job yourself but, as you're working in a confined space, ensure adequate ventilation. You'll have to work neatly and quickly or hard edges will form.

Clean the bath thoroughly and wash off all traces of soapless detergent. Tie empty jam jars under taps in case there's an occasional drip. Protect the near edge from grease of your arm with a piece of clean cloth and start at the top middle of the far side, using the best bath enamel you can buy. Work to left and right and down until you have finished that side. Then attend to ends and bottom and lastly the near side, following the same procedure as on the far side.

Allow the coating to harden for four or five days without steam collecting in the room. Then, as the finish hasn't anywhere near the wearing properties of the original glaze, which is powdered glass fused into the metal through clay undercoating at 1,000° C, you won't be able to use abrasive cleaners – just paraffin or a mild detergent. Indeed, the sole use of these cleansers will lengthen the life of a factory glazed bath considerably. In time, abrasives wear even the hardest surface.

With hand-applied bath enamels you'll have to turn on

the cold tap first when drawing water – to allow the differences in coefficients of expansion between coating and underlying metal to catch up gradually with one another.

The scaling that sometimes forms under the taps of acrylic baths may be removed with a fine metal polish. Don't use chemical bath stain removers.

Bathroom wall tiles Hard glazed ceramic tiles afford poor grip for paint. If they're starting to look dingy, new tiles can be stuck on top. Or you can buy self-adhesive sheeting in various patterns and cut to the size of the tiles. But you may not want to go to this expense; so clean them well and then swill with clean water. Leave for at least 24 hours to allow moisture absorbed by the grouting (material joining the edges) to evaporate.

Then apply two finishing coats of alkyd resin or polyurethane paint thinly – not undercoat or primer which haven't good adhesive properties.

Painting old tiles would hardly be suitable for a kitchen owing to the excessive wear it receives.

Relief painting Two tones can be applied effectively to a relief surface such as an Adam-style fire surround where the interstices can be white and the raised portions gold, or a picture frame where the lower parts are a muddy colour and the protruberances bright. Apply the muddy colour thinly all over and, when dry, brush lightly over the raised portions in the second colour with a squeezed out brush.

Another way is to coat the whole lot with the second colour, leave to dry and apply the first colour, again all over. While this first colour is still wet, wipe over the raised parts to remove it from the tops of the reliefs and leave the second in the valleys.

Cracked firehearths The crack that appears in the centre of nearly all hearths where there is an open solid fuel fire is due to unequal expansion between tiles and concrete base. When renewing them, place a sheet of Asbestolux (not ordinary asbestos which will break) between tiles and concrete and this will at least delay future cracking.

Dampen the Asbestolux to prevent harmful dust from flying and cut to size with a blunt tenon saw held obliquely (almost horizontally).

If the tiles are old and themselves cracked and difficult to replace to a perfect match, chip off the whole lot, roughen the underlying concrete with a cold chisel and hammer, paint with a PVA adhesive and trowel on a screed of mortar (about 1 part of cement, by volume, to 5 parts of fine sand). Trowel smooth.

This will dry to an objectionable grey colour, so whiten it with a donkey stone – the kind grandmother used to whiten her front doorstep. If you cannot get donkey stones, mix 1 part, by volume, of powdered glue size to 16 parts of whiting, adding boiling water until it reaches brushing consistency. This will turn brown directly in front of the fire. When this happens, spread the good part to cover the bad with a damp cloth. In time, the whole lot will need washing off and renewing – a job that doesn't take long.

A quicker alternative, but one that doesn't spread so well, is to paint with size-bound non-washable distemper, known commonly as whitewash and once used widely for ceilings but discarded in recent years owing to its failure to take any other coating on top.

Don't use emulsion paint which will turn brown the first time you light a fire, nor oil paint which will blister where heat is greatest.

Gilding and bronzing   A touch of gold adds richness to edges of shelves and on the relief portions of a raised surface.

Gilding is the application of gold leaf – which is beyond the scope of amateurs. If gold leaf is already on, don't varnish it or it'll become dull looking. Rather boil scraps of parchment in water to make a parchment size. This evens up lustre and can be washed off and renewed when it becomes dirty – and that doesn't happen frequently.

Bronzing is done with gold paint which, because of the relative heaviness of the metallic particles, requires stirring between each dip of the brush.

Bronze particles rising to the surface of the wet paint eventually become tarnished through exposure to air; so choose a finely milled gold paint which, naturally, is a little more expensive.

Even this leaves a roughish surface whereas gold leaf is perfectly smooth. You can achieve a *near* gold-leaf effect by varnishing the raw surface and, when the coating becomes tacky, rubbing in fine bronze powder.

Marbled slate mantelpiece In the last century slate would be dipped in a tank of water on the surface of which were floated pigments ground in gold size and interblended by drawing a rod through them this way and that to form whorls and other patterns. The piece would then be varnished and stoved. When marbled slate becomes damaged strip the lot with a non-caustic paint stripper and stripping knife. Work on a few inches at a time, and gently so that the slate isn't scratched.

The slate can then be remarbled by dipping hemp or tow (used by plumbers to wrap joints) in a shellac or glue solution and teasing it out to form a random stencil. Leave to dry and spray paint through that onto the surface. Experiment first on an off-cut of wood to determine the right distances between gun and stencil and between stencil and slate. An aerosol spray can also be used.

A more arduous but easier controlled way is to use scumble over a ground coat and, while still wet, scratching the design of your choice with a pointed tool. Then varnish.

Scumble was largely used in the last century and at the turn of this by craftsmen who could imitate the grains of various timbers so faithfully as to deceive timber merchants. With the advent of bright, clean colours their popularity died – and so have the men who could use them effectively.

Their advantage lies in the fact that, when applied to a ground coat, they 'stay put' and don't flow out as is the case with modern oil paints – and that is why you can use a pointed instrument to form your design.

If you ask a modern paint salesman for scumble he won't

know what you're talking about. Your builders' merchant will but he may not stock it and will have to order it.

Brass and copper fitments Clean thoroughly with metal polish, using an old toothbrush to get into enrichments. Treat obstinate stains with lemon juice or non-caustic paint remover and rub lightly with the finest steelwool you can get.

Where there's already a coating it will, no doubt, be cellulose, so rub on a cellulose thinner. If anything else, all you can do is try a non-caustic paint stripper and scrape, prodding into intricacies with a sharp-pointed knife.

Now wash in boiling soda water to remove polish and other contaminants and wash again in clean boiling water to remove the soda. Dry quickly before air can get to it and coat with clear cellulose. This won't give quite the brilliance of newly polished metal but it'll save a lot of time.

Wear cotton gloves (lintless) because the least suspicion of grease, even from what you may think is a clean hand, is inimical to cellulose.

Ebonising wood Remove old coats with non-caustic paint remover and apply three or four coats of black cellulose paint, rubbing down lightly between each and following the direction of the grain of the wood, using flour grade abrasive paper. Leave for 48 hours and rub with fine wirewool moistened with soap.

For oak, apply liberally a solution of any iron salt – made by dissolving iron sulphate in water; or soak bits of iron in vinegar and leave standing for several days; or immerse rusty nails in a jar of water for a week.

If you don't want to use cellulose on soft wood for fear of chipping, treat with a solution of tannic acid and, when dry, rub down and polish or varnish. Make your own tannic acid by boiling oak galls or oak scraps in water.

In all cases, the black improves with age.

Fumed oak Fuming was discovered by accident. In olden days, when oak was cheap and used for horses' stables, fumes from the animals' urine darkened the woodwork.

You can imitate this by putting the article in an enclosed vessel with a little ammonia in the bottom.

Hammered metal finish Coat with silicones which, when new, cause 'cissing' of subsequently applied paint and give it a beaten pewter effect.

Wrought iron finish on steel Add a little aluminium paint (not aluminium primer sealer) to a matt black oil paint; or use dark grey micaceous iron oxide paint (from builders' merchants).

Crackle finish Apply a quick-drying paint over a slow-drying undercoat to which a little linseed oil has been added. An alternative is a strong solution of powdered glue and water, or dextrine. After the crackle has formed and paint dried, apply a clear varnish.

Shot-silk effect Apply a stone-like masonry paint to produce a rough surface. Leave to dry and seal with shellac varnish before coating with neutral grey cellulose. Then, using a spray gun or aerosol paint can held at an oblique angle, apply a coat of one colour from the side, and another colour from the other side. Each microscopic bump will then be in two colours, one on each side of a bump. Varnish.

Stencilling Stencilling paper can be bought, or you can draw the design on cartridge paper. Then rub over with a rag soaked in raw linseed oil to make cutting easier. The cutting should be done on plate glass using a sharp knife. When dry, stiffen by coating both sides with shellac knotting, which also makes cleaning the edges easier. Pour a very little drop of paint on a palette and dab with the stencil brush (don't dip it in the can).

Painting iron railings Painting railings with a brush is a lengthy job and inclined to lead to 'misses'. Instead, use painters' mitts (from builders' merchants or ship's chandlers). Dip in the paint and wipe on. A pair of old gloves does equally well.

9 Painting the outside

Sequence of exterior painting is: eaves, rainwater gutters, rendering (if there is any), downpipes, windows, doors and lastly, air vents (if made of metal).

The reason for leaving downpipes, windows and doors until after the rendering is that it's easier to 'cut in' from a small area to a large than the other way about.

Eaves The undersides of eaves are so well protected that they need only the minimum of painting. Provided there are no cracks or signs of peeling you can often get away with brushing down, using a banister brush, wiping over with white spirit or substitute and giving a finishing coat.

This means climbing a ladder once only with the necessary equipment in a small bucket and shifting it along as you go.

If you *have* to remove old paint, don't use a blow lamp under eaves. Inflammable sarking (roofing felt under tiles) may be exposed here and there or there may be a collection of cobwebs and rubbish which could catch alight and smoulder for a long time before bursting into flame and causing a conflagration.

Galvanized iron gutters Scrape, chip and wirebrush off rusty patches, touch in with zinc chromate primer and give the inside two coats of black bituminous paint. This is extremely waterproof and, being so high up, won't be seen. Outside: after priming bared patches, give one undercoat and two finishing coats of the same alkyd resin paint that's being used on the woodwork.

Use this paint also on fascia boards (that hold the gutters) after cleaning and glasspapering down and touching in bare patches with wood primer. A radiator brush will come in handy for reaching parts behind the gutter.

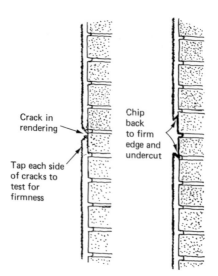

Crack in rendering

Tap each side of cracks to test for firmness

Chip back to firm edge and undercut

Fig. 29

Asbestos gutters After wetting thoroughly to prevent flying dust, wirebrush the whole surface to remove algae and touch in remaining green scum with ordinary household bleach diluted with 4 parts of water. Leave for 48 hours and wash off. This will kill embedded spores. Then give two coats of bituminous paint inside and a well-thinned coat of emulsion of colour to match the fascia board outside, followed by a normal coat (see page 88).

Plastic gutters Being self-coloured, these don't need paint; but if you wish to make a change rub hard with white spirit (turpentine substitute) and fine waterproof abrasive paper wetted with the spirit. Then apply two finishing coats of alkyd resin paint. No undercoat.

Wooden gutters Lined with lead and sometimes found on old properties, these should need no treatment inside. If the lead has perished, renew the entire gutter with plastic or aluminium.

Aluminium gutters One-third of the weight of iron gutters. Unlike plastic and asbestos, these will take the weight of a ladder resting against them. Delivered pre-painted, but can be over-painted if different colour desired.

Smooth rendering Don't use detergent in the water with which you wash down the surface or there may be efflorescence troubles. Brush with clear water and a stiff yard broom. Treat mossy patches as for asbestos gutters.

Scrape out cracks until you reach a firm edge. Tap the surroundings with the handle of your trowel to make sure they *are* firm. A hollow sound will indicate that the rendering has parted company from the bricks.

Undercut the firm edge (Fig. 29), wet the crack by flinging water in with a large brush, and trowel in mortar no stronger than that of the surroundings. A fairly safe mix is 1 part of cement to 6 parts of sharp sand, with a little plasticiser added to make working easier. As mortar shrinks on drying, do this job in two or three operations, leaving each application to dry.

Now brush on the sealer recommended by the manufacturer of the masonry finish you're applying, using a 100 mm (4 in.) nylon brush or roller (pages 25 and 27), and, when dry, follow with the finish which can either resemble stone or be perfectly smooth. The latter won't pick up dirt so readily and will be easier to clean. See reference to *paint scuttle* on page 27.

A cement paint is not advisable because it dries so hard and readily cracks with structural movement. An outdoor grade of emulsion paint can be used for a cheap job but it won't last as long as a properly formulated masonry paint.

Roughcast rendering (small stones mixed with mortar) The extra long pile roller mentioned on page 27 is the quickest way to apply a smooth masonry paint; but sealing is best done with a brush, the filling being nylon.

Cracks should be undercut and stopped up with mortar imitating the surrounding roughness by placing a board over the wet surface and pulling away smartly.

Tyrolean finish This resembles roughcast but has no pebbles. It consists of mortar applied by a special gun. Cracks can be stopped and finished off in the same way as roughcast. Rub down any sharp points that may protrude.

Pebbledash (small pebbles flung onto wet mortar) As the pebbles are exposed, they form their own decoration, and masonry paint need be applied only if the pebbles become loose or their surface tatty-looking. Unfortunately this happens all too often when shrinkage of the mortar causes haircracks to develop round each pebble. Rain enters, freezes in cold weather and expands to push the rendering off in particles.

When pebbledash develops a bad crack, undercut and stop up with mortar. While still wet fling on pebbles to match the existing ones, using a hand shovel.

Limewash It is difficult to get any other type of paint to adhere over limewash, though some masonry paints are advertised to do just that, provided the existing limewash is well weathered. Limewash can also be used on stucco, the rendering often used on houses built in the 1800s.

The material is easy to slosh on with a grass or pure nylon brush, after cleaning down well. Recipes for making your own limewash are given in chapter 1.

Downpipes (Metal, plastic or asbestos). Treat in the same way as is described under the heading of rainwater gutters.

To prevent paint splashing onto bricks or a newly-painted wall, insert a sheet of cardboard, about 460 mm × 760 mm (18 in. × 2 ft 6 in.), behind the pipe and move it down as you go (Fig. 30).

Don't bother about the inside of the pipe. But perfectionists will drop a rope, with a stout weight attached to one end, down the pipe, knot a ball of cloth round the other end to fit the aperture (but not to jam in it), pull down a little way, pour bituminous paint through the top and then pull the rope down and up several times.

With an old pipe, preparatory internal cleaning is done with a ball of wirewool before using cloth.

Fig. 30

Windows and doors These have already been dealt with in chapter 7. Give two finishing coats to achieve the minimum 0.127 mm (5/1,000 in.) thickness needed for extra protection against weather.

It would be sacrilege to paint an oak door. Linseed oil on its own isn't good enough. It's apt to remain sufficiently sticky to attract dust; a madison sealer, which is a refinement, is better but still becomes dirty. To clean such surfaces, apply white spirit (turpentine substitute) with a coarse cloth. A soap pad is also effective.

Ordinary wood varnish is of no use at all when exposed to the sun's rays and will last little longer than 12 months. Polyurethane and yacht varnishes are little better. What is needed is an ultra-violet ray resisting varnish which has a life of at least five years.

Metal air vents Remove rust, touch in with zinc chromate primer and apply undercoat and two finishing coats. Make sure the vents aren't choked with cobwebs.

Garden sheds

If made of wood, sheds may be painted either to match the decor of the house or in green to camouflage it among surrounding foliage.

For resinous cedars, prime with aluminium primer sealer and follow with two finishing coats of an alkyd resin paint. There's no need for undercoating if you use this sealer. An alternative is a tinted proprietary wood preservative which will give colour and also show the grain through.

The wood will no doubt be unplaned and this roughness will give excellent adhesion so that paintwork will last twice as long as that on the house.

For teak, which is cheap in some tropical countries, use a teak sealer instead of aluminium primer sealer under paint.

In Britain and other western countries all good timbers are becoming increasingly expensive and so cheap wood used in prefabricated sheds is often coated in the factory with a plastic. This doesn't need painting. Its chief drawback is that, if damaged by the fall of a garden tool against it, rain enters and destroys adhesion or causes rot. All you can do is to touch up damaged parts with paint.

Roofs of sheds are generally of timber with a bituminous felt covering. When this gets dingy wirebrush off mossy growths and treat with household bleach diluted with 4 parts of water and washed off after 48 hours. Then brush over with bituminous paint which can be venetian red to resemble tiles, or green.

The roofing timbers may not be sufficiently strong to bear your weight. That is where the striker (page 22) comes in for reaching the ridge.

Wet the surface of asbestos sheds to guard your lungs from deadly dust and wear a face mask when wirebrushing before repainting. Green patches will need the household bleach treatment mentioned previously. Then give the roof two coats of bituminous paint, and the side walls, which don't get the full force of sun and rain, a well-thinned coat of outdoor grade emulsion of the same colour as the remainder of the house. Follow this with a normal coat. An oil paint direct on asbestos is of no use as it will turn soapy.

Seaside property

Being highly hygroscopic, salt attracts moisture which, as we have already seen, will cause paint to peel.

A salty atmosphere is almost as bad, and so houses close to the sea will need repainting twice as often as those inland. You can lengthen the life of paintwork by washing down extra thoroughly before starting work. Choose a calm day or one when a breeze is blowing away from the land towards the sea. Do this washing down between each coat you apply.

Touching up once a year will save no end of time required for a complete repaint.

10 Climbing aloft

Folding ladders can be tucked away comfortably between jobs. Unfolded to their fullest extent they'll reach the eaves of a bungalow but not of a storeyed house. With various permutations of unfolding they can be used to reach a ceiling or high stairwell.

A portable scaffolding tower will reach the top of a two-floor house and is the safest and most convenient form of climbing heights, affording wider space for movement and holding tools. Fit toe boards all round the top platform to prevent your feet from slipping through. The tower consists of metal parts readily clamped together and taken apart for storage. Some are fitted with rubber feet and others have small wheels with brakes – which enable them to be easily moved round the house without reassembly.

As with a folding ladder, the tower can be adapted for stairs and lesser heights.

Towers are expensive to buy or hire from a builders' hire service; and, if you're hiring, you'll have to take a gamble with the weather.

Ladders

Most householders will rely on a ladder.

Pole ladders are long and in one piece, the stiles (uprights) being joined with dowel-shaped *rounds* of about 25 mm (1 in.) diameter. These are used by builders and aren't suitable for amateurs because of weight and storage difficulties. You should get an extension ladder whose stiles are joined by rectangular *rungs*. Two sections are generally sufficient for a two-floor house and three for a three-floor house.

The former can be slid up and down by hand. The latter needs a rope and pulleys.

When taken apart these ladders can be slung over the tie

beams of a garage or outhouse where air can circulate. If you have no such outhouse, drive three stout square-nosed staples into the mortar jointing of the house, on a side wall where they won't be an eyesore, and hang the sections horizontally over them. The middle staple prevents sagging. Rope round a protective sheet of polythene or a tarpaulin, but leave the underside free for ventilation (Fig. 31). Always padlock a ladder to wherever it's being stored or you'll present burglars with a free entry to your home.

Use creosote to preserve a wooden ladder – not paint which will hide any defects that may develop.

An aluminium extension ladder which, of course, will not need creosote, is three times stronger and a third the weight of a wooden one; but it will cost twice as much. The disadvantage is that metal is inclined to slip more than wood and so it'll have to be secured extra firmly when in use.

The parts of an extension can be carried horizontally or near vertically as is shown in Fig. 32. Note the tilt and position of the hands which preserve centre of balance.

To extend a ladder, judge the height you want, place one end against the wall and grasp the other end. Now walk towards the wall, shifting the hands from rung to rung, as you go. When upright, pull out the foot one unit away from the wall for every four in height (Fig. 33).

This method requires strength. So, if you can get help, stand the bottom of the ladder at the proper distance from the wall and get your colleague to put his foot on the bottom rung while you elevate the top as already described.

Yet another way is to stand one closed section near the wall, but not touching it, pull the top out a little way and slide the other section up as far as you can reach. Mount a few rungs, jerk the ladder out and push up still higher. And so on.

Once the ladder is extended you can move it a few feet either way by joggling it along the wall, alternately at top and bottom, *a little at a time.*

Protect paving stones underneath against spillages of paint with an old bedsheet. Don't use polythene; it's slippery.

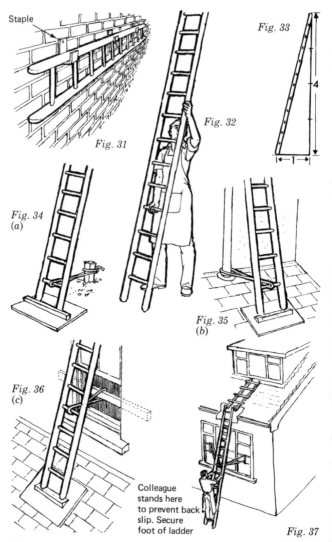

Staple

Fig. 31

Fig. 32

Fig. 33

4

1

Fig. 34
(a)

Fig. 35
(b)

Fig. 36
(c)

Colleague
stands here
to prevent back
slip. Secure
foot of ladder

Fig. 37

Minimum overlap of the sections *when the ladder is fully extended* is two rungs for a *closed* length of up to 5 m (16 ft), three rungs for up to 6 m (17 to 20 ft) and four for ladders whose closed length measures 6.5 m (21 ft) and over.

Ladder attachments For sloped ground you can buy an extension stirrup which can be clamped onto one of the stiles. A ladder stay, which is attached to an upper rung, and rests against the wall, will be needed to reach rainwater gutters of widely overhanging eaves such as are seen in many hot countries.

In any case, it's unwise to rest a ladder against a gutter. If it's made of iron, the weight may loosen the brackets. If plastic, it will bend. If asbestos it may break. Where you *must* use a gutter as a support, protect it with a sack filled with old clothes as is shown in Fig. 37.

Ladder safety Get a colleague to stand on the bottom rung while you're working aloft. Otherwise you'll have to resort to one of the methods (not all) shown in Figs. 34, 35 and 36.

Drive a stake into cultivated ground (a), firm the soil and stand the foot on a plank of wood with a lip nailed on midway. On paving, drive wedges under the ladder feet (b); *or* secure to a convenient house projection, such as a downpipe; *or*, if there's a convenient window, open it and tie to a broomstick or length of batten resting against the inside of the wall (c).

Mounting a ladder The 'whip' of a ladder will frighten a lot of people, but if it had no 'give' the ladder would snap – so would the Eiffel Tower if it didn't sway slightly!

A fireman will grasp the stiles so that he can slide down if anything untoward happens. A decorator generally grasps the rungs. Do whatever you find most handy.

Lace shoes securely. Don't wear wellington boots which could be dangerous. Tuck overall bottoms into your socks and see that no loose clothing is flapping about.

Carry paint, brushes, scrapers, cleaning cloths and glasspaper in a small bucket or bag which can be hooked

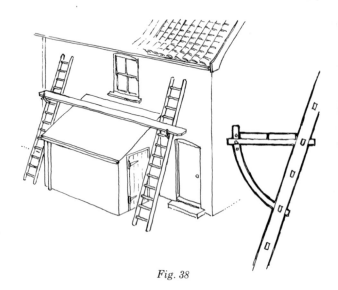

Fig. 38

onto an upper rung with a meat hook. Never carry sharp instruments in your pockets in case of the millionth chance of an accident.

An experienced man will run up and down a ladder like a hamster. Don't do that. Climb step by step, keeping your eyes fixed on the wall immediately facing you. If you look up or down you may become giddy.

On reaching the top, lash it to a gutter or convenient gutter bracket. Keep the centre of your body balance over the ladder; don't lean over too far. If right-handed, work from right to left; if left-handed, from left to right.

Now you're protected against falls and both outward and sideways slip.

Reaching a dormer window Fig. 37 shows how to reach a dormer window. The cat ladder, which can be bought and cut to the required length, or made yourself by nailing battens together, is lashed to one part of an extension ladder.

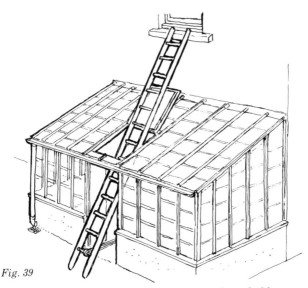

Fig. 39

To reach the ridge (top) of a sloping roof, cat ladders are obtainable with hooks which engage on the ridge tiles.

Reaching above a lean-to Before having an extension to your house built, consider how you're going to reach that part of the house immediately above. It would be convenient to have a flat roof (which is not actually flat but slightly sloped away from the house) and make sure that the roof rafters are sufficiently strong to take a ladder and bear your weight.

Where the lean-to is already in existence and has a pitched roof (sloping), and isn't too wide, stand one half of an extension ladder against one side of the house wall and the other extension against the other side. Join up with scaffold planks by means of cripples (Fig. 38).

Minimum thicknesses of scaffold planks of usual width for various spans are: 50 mm (2 in.) for 2.5 m (8 ft 6 in.) long; 38 mm (1½ in.) for 1.5 m (5 ft); and 31.75 mm (1¼ in.) for 1 m (3 ft 3 in.). Wherever possible, place two 225 mm (9 in.) wide planks side-by-side to afford sufficient standing room.

For a glass-roofed conservatory, take out one or two of the roofing panes, make a hinged wooden frame and replace the glass within the frame. You can then open this 'skylight' and poke a ladder up through the opening (Fig. 39). Don't forget to leave sufficient room for your body as well as the ladder to pass through the aperture. Without first consulting the writer, a friend made his opening, got the ladder and his head up – but the rest of him wouldn't follow!

Interior heights

There's no awkward height that cannot be reached with thought and ingenuity.

Room When dealing with the ceiling of a very large room, the quickest job is done by hiring scaffold planks and four trestles. Stand one trestle in each corner of the room and join each couple on the long side with two planks side-by-side, supporting the middle over boxes of the right height.

Place planks across and you can walk backwards and forwards at will. These movable planks can then be slid along the side planks as you go (Fig. 40).

For a medium sized room or entrance hall, place one end of a plank on a stout wooden box of height to bring your head some 150 mm (6 in.) from the ceiling. Stand the other end on an appropriate step of household steps (Fig. 41).

For a very small room, you can often get away with household steps with a slight adaptation. Cut a rebate on one side of the top step to take a batten which can be bolted to the stile and secured temporarily with a wing nut (Fig. 42).

You can now steady yourself with one hand and a screw hook inserted into the top of the batten will hold paint kettle or other clobber.

For an extremely high ceiling in an old house (3 or 4 m, which is 12 ft or over), stand one half of an extension ladder against each wall and join up with a plank, supporting the middle if necessary. Rough-nail battens at the foot of the ladders and protect the walls with plywood (Fig. 43).

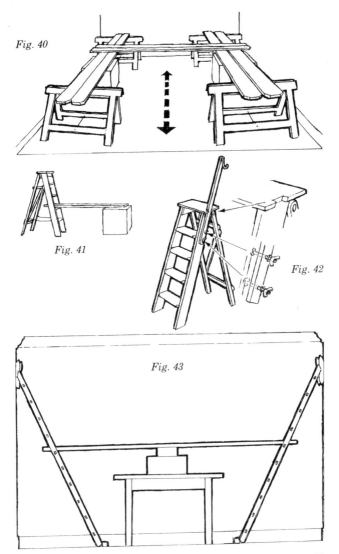

Fig. 40

Fig. 41

Fig. 42

Fig. 43

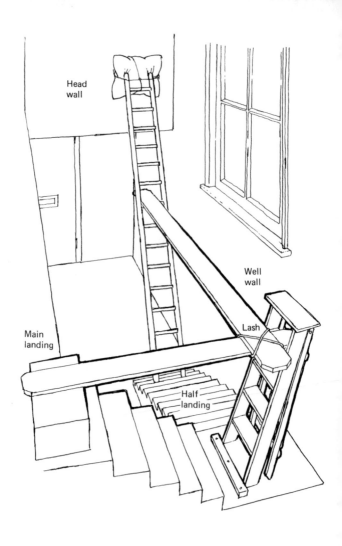

Head wall

Well wall

Lash

Main landing

Half landing

Fig. 44

Stairwell If you have no folding ladder or portable scaffold tower to reach the upper parts of a high stairwell, adopt the device shown in Fig. 44.

Stand one half of an extension ladder against a convenient stair riser and lean it against the head wall. As this wall will probably be of wallboard attached to concealed studs (wooden upright supports) or of lath and plaster also attached to studs, distribute the weight by inserting a short piece of thin wood or ply so that it bridges the studs.

Close a step ladder and stand it on the half-landing, leaning against the well wall. The stair carpet will have to be removed; so rough-nail a batten on the floor of the half-landing immediately in front of the bottom of the stiles of the step ladder to prevent its slipping.

Turn a stout wooden box of convenient height upside-down on the top landing and join up to the appropriate step of the step ladder with planks. Join up that end of the planks with more planks to a rung of the extension ladder. Lash these joins for safety.

Where stairs have a twist instead of a square half-landing, stand a small box, of the same height as the riser, on the tread immediately below to increase width to hold the step ladder.

With spiral stairs, there's often a window in the well wall, the window board (ledge) of which can be joined up to the opposing window board of a room opposite.

Cut this plank to fit precisely and keep it for this job alone.

11 Wall coverings

What a bewildering array of wall coverings there are!

Apart from printed and strippable papers, there are stiffened embossed pulp (which can be overpainted or varnished), waterproof papers, polyethylene film (such as Novamura), metallics and coverings that are brushed on like paint, and also those made of flock and cork.

They're sold in varying sizes. That's why there's no better way of estimating the amount required for a room than that on page 57.

Wallpapers

The better the quality of paper the easier it is to hang and match. Cheap papers tear easily.

For very small rooms choose a free match (small nondescript pattern) and the room will look larger. These sometimes vary in tone from edge to edge, but mostly alternate rolls may be reversed without the reversal being noticed, dark side butting onto dark side and lighter onto light.

A medium sized room can take a medium sized pattern and in one that is very large you can indulge in all manner of William Morris designs.

As one drop (cut length ready for hanging) has to butt on to the preceding one, there'll naturally be more wastage with a large design than a small one. You can however (and if the paper has a set pattern) save by cutting from two rolls at once. These will readily match up without undue cutting. Real waste comes with a drop pattern where a second drop has to be slid up or down to coincide (Fig. 45).

With a flower pattern which leaves doubt as to which way up it goes, cutting into lengths may get them mixed up; so note where the printed shadows from the flowers fall. These should face downwards.

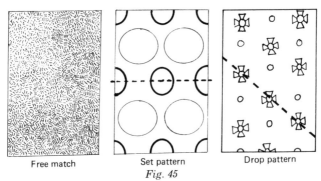

| Free match | Set pattern | Drop pattern |

Fig. 45

The first job is to 'shade' the rolls. That is, see that the printing is even in tone from one roll to another. Sometimes they vary owing to imperfections in the printing process. Drape several rolls over the back of a settee and stand back to take a look. Any that are lighter or darker can be reserved for another wall and the discrepancy won't be noticed.

If there's a selvedge (unprinted margin at each side), it should be trimmed off; or you can get the wallpaper shop to do it for you. This trimming should be carried out accurately or the patterns won't match and in struggling to achieve a perfect butt join, you'll get bulges and creases.

Surface preparation Strip existing wallpaper by brushing with water generously all round the room. Then brush round again with more water, this time using a stripping knife (Fig. 4, page 30). Wash off all traces of old size.

A waterproof or varnished paper won't allow water to penetrate to the paste; so scrape the surface with an old hacksaw blade, coarse glasspaper or other abrading tool or material, and use a chemical wallpaper remover. Don't hang new paper over an existing one because the old paste will be nearing the end of its useful life and additional weight will bring the lot off.

You may think, why then can you stick lining paper on a chancey wall and paper over that? The answer is that in this case the paste is new. Lining paper is often used under

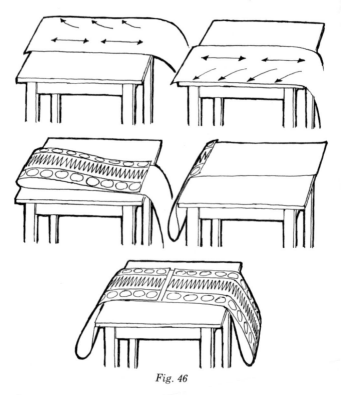

Fig. 46

heavy and special papers and, when this is essential, manufacturer's instructions will say so.

You have washed off old size, so now resize to satisfy and even up porosity, by brushing on a *weak* solution of the adhesive you're using. As a rule, decorators don't size a previously emulsioned surface because emulsion itself acts as a seal, and too much water will weaken the bond of the emulsion and may also cause crazing. But sizing will help you to slide the paper into position over such a rough surface. In this case, instead of ordinary size, use a thinned alkyd resin varnish or any thinned light-coloured oil paint

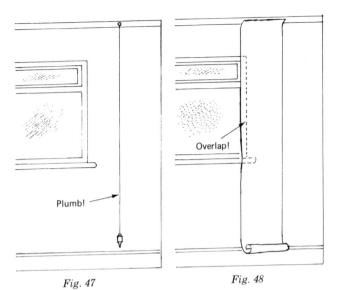

Fig. 47 Fig. 48

you happen to have over from a previous job. The paint will have to be strained so that 'nibs' don't show through as bumps in the paper.

While the size is drying, cut sufficient lengths to cover one wall, adding 100 mm (4 in.) to the height of the wall.

Pasting and hanging Papers you paste yourself hold more securely to an uneven wall than those already pasted which only need wetting.

Lay a length of paper on the pasting table, pattern side down, to line up with the far side of the table and with one end abutting its edge. Paste with criss-cross strokes down the centre; then brush out towards the farther edge so that no paste creeps under to mar the pattern.

Now slide the paper to the near side of the table and paste towards you (Fig. 46).

Fold this part of the pasted paper over so that it nearly meets the unpasted part. Move it along with the fold hanging down and continue pasting the other half. Fold

103

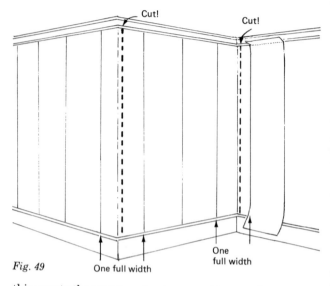

Cut! Cut!

Fig. 49   One full width   One full width

this over to the centre and put on one side to soak while you paste the next length.

After pasting the second length, the first should be ready for hanging. Thick papers requiring longer soaking time will say so on their instructions.

As windows, doors and wall corners are seldom at right-angles to the floor and ceiling, plumb the wall at one side of the window, at a distance a little less than the width of the paper. Chalk the string with white or coloured chalk, according to the colour of the substratum, and attach it at the top – or get somebody to hold it there – while you grasp the bob tightly and snap the string against the wall to leave a chalk mark. A large nut or other small weight makes a good plumb bob (Fig. 47).

Loop the first length of paper over your arm, mount a step ladder and, holding the top to overlap junction of wall and ceiling by about 50 mm (2 in.), smooth it down with a smoothing brush (Fig. 1, page 23) to line up with the chalk mark. It will now overlap the window frame slightly.

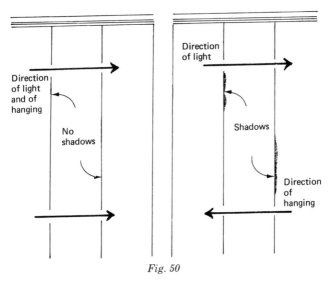

Fig. 50

Crease with the back of the scissors or shears along the juncture of wall and ceiling (or picture rail), peel back and cut at the crease mark. Brush back the paper. Repeat at the bottom where it overlaps skirting board (base board); also peel back the paper adjoining window frame and trim there (Fig. 48).

Carry on, butting each drop neatly up to the preceding one.

A perfectionist will now use a seam roller which is narrow and, when applied over two abutting edges of hung paper, will ensure perfect adhesion at such a weak point. Place a length of toilet paper under the roller to prevent 'polishing' the surface of the paper. A seam roller shouldn't be used on an embossed paper or it will flatten out the high parts.

After hanging the last drop before reaching an external corner, measure the distance to the corner and add 50 mm (2 in.).

Paste and cut the next length *longitudinally* to this

105

measurement and hang that – to turn the corner by 50 mm. Then plumb the wall again and hang the off-cut up to this chalk mark (Fig. 49).

Follow a similar procedure with internal corners – though about 10 mm ($\frac{3}{8}$ in.) will do for the turn-round in this instance. If you don't plumb the wall at this point, irregularities may cause the top of a patterned paper to go awry where it meets the ceiling, and you'll get bulges and creases if you attempt to put the fault right.

In spite of this safeguard there may be misalignment close to the ceiling. This is because the ceiling slopes, and even a small slope will look ugly. If your room is like this, the only thing you can do is to choose a paper without a prominent pattern.

And so you will eventually reach the door. Stop there and restart at the other side of the window, again working towards the door.

Why start at the window? First, because an uneven wall is bound to cause overlapping in places. However slight the overlaps are, no shadows will be cast. Shadows will, however, show up as dark streaks at the joins if you work from door to window (Fig. 50). The second reason is that off-cuts can be used over a door where slight mismatching won't be noticed. Off-cuts can also be used under windows where they are in a poor light and hidden by curtains (Fig. 51).

Chimney breast Exception to the rule of papering away from the strongest source of light is when dealing with a chimney breast. Here, for appearance sake, hang one length of a set patterned paper dead centre and work towards the window until you reach the first interior corner. A drop patterned paper is best hung on either side of the centre dividing line – to preserve a better balance (Fig. 52). Any slight mismatch at the internal corner will be hidden by furniture standing in the alcove. Shadows cast at the joins on the chimney breast by working backwards will be slight because the height of the wall above the mantelpiece is only half that of the full height, and so there'll be only half the possible wall bulges.

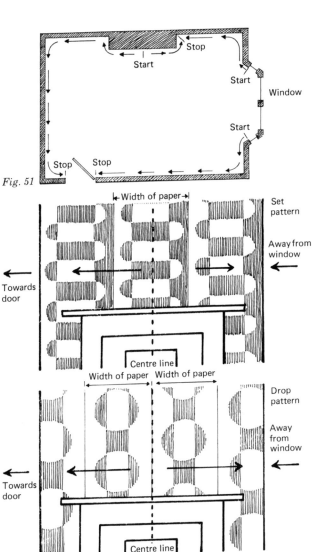

Fig. 51

Fig. 52

Carry on at the other side of the centre drop as usual (Fig. 51). Keep a damp cloth handy to wipe off exuding paste from all paintwork because paste has a contracting action which causes cracking of the paintfilm.

Electric light switches Turn off the current at the mains on reaching a wall switch. You can now remove the switch plate and trim the paper to stick under before replacing the plate.

But a professional won't touch the plate. He will hang the pasted drop on the wall and make a mark where a bulge reveals the switch knob. Then he will pull back the paper to this point, cut for a small distance diagonally in both directions, press back the paper and crease round the plate, peel back again and trim to these creases. He will now give a final smooth down and the trimming cuts won't show (Fig. 53).

Doorcases On approaching the door, roughcut the drop to the shape of the doorcase and slightly oversize. Hang the pasted drop, crease round the juncture of wall and door, peel back and trim – in a way similar to that adopted for a window frame.

Other wall coverings

Instructions for handling coverings other than paper are given by the manufacturer. With some products, the wall has to be pasted, not the paper, and subsequent removal requires different techniques. Special adhesives may also have to be used and perhaps the wall lined with lining paper. Here are a few of the better known unusual coverings!

Aluminium foil Used for hiding obstinate stains such as round a chimney breast. This sheeting is coated on the back with a synthetic rubber-based thermo-softening adhesive and so has to be stuck on with a hot domestic iron and then rolled. Hang lining paper on top to prevent condensation on such a hard, non-porous surface; or it can be painted over as an alternative to wallpaper.

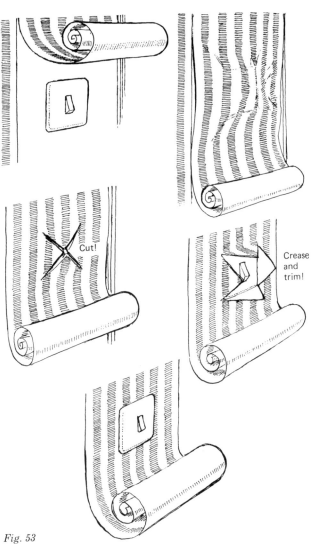

Cut!

Crease
and
trim!

Fig. 53

109

Anaglypta Made from laminated wood pulp. For high relief sheeting, use Dextrine as an adhesive. Knife it on only those parts in contact with the underlying surface. In no circumstances should the reliefs be filled. Hold in position with fine panel pins until the adhesive has set. Can be emulsion-painted and then given a coat of eggshell varnish.

Flock coverings, canvas and jute Should be trimmed with a sharp knife and straight edge. The wall must be lined first. Scrupulous cleanliness is essential as the surface easily gets soiled. Smooth down with a roller – not a smoothing brush.

'Frosted-glass' imitation A transparent self-adhesive covering for bathroom and water closet windows. Appearance is that of real frosted glass.

Grass cloth Cracks readily so fold very loosely when carrying a cut length to the wall. Trim with steel straight edge and curved knife. Use hot-water paste and don't oversoak. Smooth down with a felt-covered roller. As the rolls tend to vary considerably in colour, pay special attention to preliminary shading (page 101). Even then, joins are bound to show, so hide with strip borders.

Lead foil An alternative to pitch paper. Paste with a mixture of gold size and white lead and overlap the edges; don't attempt to butt-join. Coat with a matt paint to provide 'grip' for lining paper which should be hung on top.

Lincrusta In the same family as Anaglypta but made of paper coated with a putty-like composition. Can be overpainted and subsequent stippling with a brush gives an even all-over tone.

Lining paper Used for doubtful surfaces and also under heavy wall coverings. Inexpensive and can be bought in various tints. Stick it on horizontally; that is, at right-angles to a subsequently hung wall covering. But if you wish to use it as a base for emulsion paint, hang vertically leaving about 0.5 mm (1/32 in.) gap between each drop; otherwise slight inadvertent overlaps will show through the paint. There's no need to apply size over lining paper if you're going to wallpaper over.

Painted-on wall covering More of a paint than a proper wall covering, though it gives the rich variegated effect of an expensive paper. Disadvantage: cannot be washed – only vacuum-cleaned.

Pitch paper An alternative to aluminium or lead foil, or aluminium primer sealer (page 39) for sealing stains to hold the stain back. Before sticking on, dampen the paper side to prevent blistering, and use a stiff paste on the pitch side. Don't trim off selvedge but slightly overlap each piece.

Polystyrene sheeting Used for insulation under wall-paper to minimise condensation. 2 mm to 5 mm gauge.

Quilted covering Generally made of P.V.C. Used for covering bedheads, doors, baby's cots and as window drapes.

Sanitary wallpapers Printed in oil paints, not the customary watercolours. Useful for steamy atmospheres and are often varnished after hanging. Not easily obtainable.

Vinyl coverings Some have a paper backing and others not. When the former are stripped (which can be done 'dry' by lifting at one corner with a knife and pulling) the paper is left behind and can be used in place of a lining paper. A special vinyl adhesive is needed.

Waterproof papers These are useful for bathrooms, though they are difficult to remove without first scratching the surface and using a chemical wallpaper stripper. Disadvantage: if used on a wall that is at all inclined to be damp, they will drive the moisture to an upstairs room by capillary attraction.

Fire hazard with polystyrene tiles

Polystyrene tiles shouldn't be used immediately over a cooking stove because of the risk of pans catching alight – not even the fireproof variety unless they are coated with a fire-retarding paint. Their danger lies in their melting and falling on a wooden floor to set it alight. Oil paint shouldn't be used direct on the tiles or it will cause their disintegration. If you wish to use oil paint, though this is unwise as oil intensifies fire hazard, emulsion first. Note: the fire-retarding tiles merely *retard* the spread of a conflagration until the fire brigade arrives; they aren't fire *resistant*.

Spread the recommended adhesive over the whole of the back of a tile, not just in four blobs as is sometimes recommended. This prevents air hollows.

12 And now for the ceilings

Emulsion paint (latex) is mostly used on ceilings, as its application presents fewer problems than paper or other wall covering. You can get whatever colour you want and, for the high ceiling of a large room, a lighter shade of that predominating the floor covering is ideal. For the usual three-bedroom type of house white is the best choice.

You may, however, prefer to use paper or a stiff embossed pulp because of roughness of the surface and, for the same reason, you could apply a lining paper and emulsion paint over it.

To estimate how much paper to buy, follow a similar procedure to that of papering a wall. Offer a roll horizontally to the ceiling and at right-angles to the window and mark where the end comes. Shift the roll along and make another mark – and so on until the far end of the room is reached. Add an extra roll for wastage.

More still will be required where there's a frieze between a cornice and a picture rail. Paint cornice and picture rail first and allow to dry and harden before starting papering. Wipe off exuding paste.

As more water will drip off than soak in, use a chemical paint remover to strip old existing paper; and, if the paper is of the coated type, scuff the surface first. Wash off old size and then resize. If the surface has previously been emulsioned, use a well-thinned alkyd varnish or old strained light-coloured paint (page 46).

The ceiling of an old house may have been whitewashed. Take off the whole lot with ammonia and water, and scrape (page 15).

Clear the room as described on page 35 and cover the floor with old bedsheets. This is particularly important with vinyl flooring or linoleum which so easily marks. Switch off electric light at the mains and remove fittings.

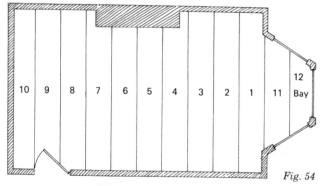

Fig. 54

Rake out cracks, stop up proud with cellulose filler and sand level when dry.

Where there's no cornice, a crack may appear and reappear at the junction of walls and ceiling owing to shrinkage and structural movement. This is best hidden with a toughened-pulp or plaster cornice which can be bought in strips. Cut the corners at an angle of 45° and if, owing to irregularities, they show a gap, stop up with filler.

Fig. 54 shows a room with a bay window. You will notice that the order of papering in the bay is a reversal of that followed on the remainder. Shadows through slight overlaps won't be noticeable here because light from the window strikes up almost vertically.

Procedure

Cut lengths of paper to the width of the room plus 100 mm (4 in.).

The gadget shown in Fig. 55 saves no end of neck-aching work. Skarsten make it in Britain. Householders in other countries will, no doubt, be able to get something similar. It consists of a spring-loaded pole which grips ceiling and floor through tension of the spring. A small platform is fixed near the top to carry a concertina of paper, leaving both hands free for working.

To do the job the orthodox way, paste each length as described in the last chapter but, instead of looping the

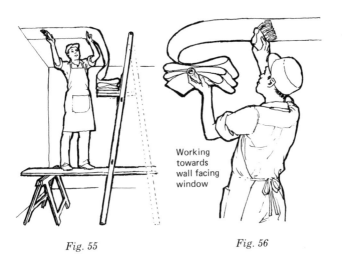

Working towards wall facing window

Fig. 55 *Fig. 56*

pasted lengths towards the centre, fold concertina-wise in about 380 mm (15 in.) folds and support it over a wooden batten or cardboard tube (Fig. 56).

Start at the window, draw a chalk line across the room 25 mm (1 in.) less than the width of the paper, using either a straight edge or chalked string.

Facing away from the window so that you can see what you're doing and starting at one side, fold back 50 mm (2 in.) of the end of the paper, pasted-side out so that the wall won't become marked. Brush this crease into the juncture of wall and ceiling and smooth out the rest of the length as you go, butting the outward side of the paper up to the chalk line.

This will leave some 50 mm overlap at the other end which should also be creased back. Crease the side of the paper adjoining the window, peel back at this side and also at the ends, and trim. Give a final brush over.

Continue towards the end of the room. If you make a mistake, peel off the length as far as the fault and restick correctly. But don't be too fussy because visitors seldom look up.

Fig. 57

The use of a seam roller is more important on a ceiling than on a wall because of the weight of the paper; but, as with a wall, don't use it over an embossed paper.

On nearing the end of the room, measure the distance to the wall facing the window, add 25 mm (1 in.) or so, cut the paper lengthways to this measurement and stick; then crease at the juncture of wall and ceiling, peel back at ends and side abutting wall, trim and restick to make a snug fit.

Electric light fittings

Treat an electric light rose in the centre of a ceiling in a way similar to that of a wall switch.

Turn the power off at the mains, remove the bulb and cut a hole in the paper to pass the flex through. Then, if it's a circular rose, cut lengthways, across and diagonally, crease the paper round, peel back, cut and resmooth.

In very old houses with high ceilings there's often a relief ornamentation encircling the rose and extending some 250 mm or as much as 600 mm (10 to 24 in.).

Suppose the enrichment comprises oak leaves as is shown in Fig. 57. Paint the enrichment first and allow to dry. Then stick the pasted paper over it and cut round with a sharp knife. Remove the unwanted circle of paper and sponge off any paste marring the ornamentation. Restick.

Improvised scaffolding to reach such a height is shown in Figs. 40 to 43, page 97).

13 Papering awkward surfaces

The time for pasted wallpaper to soak before hanging should be approximately the same for each length, so that the degree of stretching is equal.

The degree of shrinking after hanging and drying will also then be equal and patterns will fall accurately in position. That applies to walls and ceilings of a rectangular room where the weight of paper and paste is the same for each length.

Stairwell

But patterns on a stairwell could easily be thrown out of alignment by the extra weight of the longest length – that at the juncture of head and well wall being greater than the shorter lengths near and at the top of the stairs (Fig. 58).

To counteract this, the assistance of a colleague will be needed to support the bottom of the longest drop while you smooth out at the top.

Cutting Start by cutting the bottom of each length to the angle of the stairs, allowing 50 mm (2 in.) overlap, and the same also at the top. Fold these overlaps inwards to prevent paste from marring paintwork at top and bottom. Roughly smooth down, crease into the joins with the back of your scissors, peel back, cut at crease marks and resmooth.

To estimate how much paper will be required, reduce the triangular section of the well wall above the stairs to a rectangle by counting the number of steps and dividing by 2 (Fig. 13, page 55). Other walls – landing and entrance hall – being already rectangular, will present no such problem. Add an extra roll for wastage and two extra rolls if the paper has a drop pattern.

Procedure Chalk the string of a plumb bob and hold it

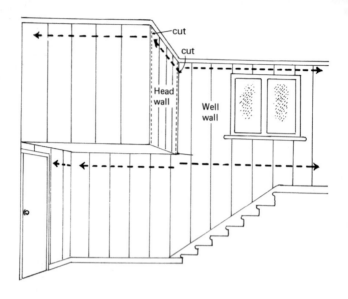

cut

cut

Head wall

Well wall

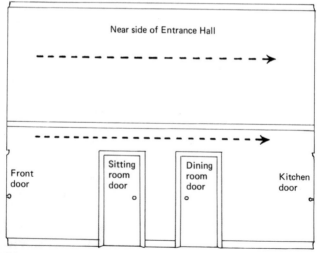

Near side of Entrance Hall

Front door

Sitting room door

Dining room door

Kitchen door

Fig. 58

against the well wall at a distance from the head wall of the width of a roll, less about 10 mm (⅜ in.). Hang the first drop there to line up with the chalk mark, as is described in detail on page 104. Slit at the bottom of the head wall and stick the overlap to the head wall.

Hang the next drop abutting this, and so on, working towards the inside of the house.

Now start at the other side of the first drop and round the head wall towards the front landing door or window. Paper over this door or window with full widths. Finally paper the facing return walls, working towards the back of the house. Paper over the top of the side bedroom doors upstairs and dining- and sitting-room doors downstairs with full widths.

This complicated explanation is best demonstrated by referring to Fig. 58.

The procedure may have to be modified according to the plan of the house but, if you're worried about some drops of paper being hung the wrong way round, don't forget that guests will be so occupied with greetings on arrival that they won't notice shadows being cast by irregularities in the wall surface. And, if there happens to be a well-wall window, as is shown in the illustration, the light coming from it will roughly equal that from the front, so that the problem will equal itself out.

Before starting work, remove stair carpet, and, when relaying after completion of the job, move it up or down a few inches, say 100 to 150 mm (4 to 6 in.) to even out wear. With a pile carpet, don't turn it top to bottom or the pile will run the wrong way and scuffing of feet will play havoc with it. This may not happen with a corded carpet but, as there are so many different kinds, check up with the carpet shop before buying.

Protecting bared stairs by merely throwing an old bedsheet over them could cause accidents through your misjudging a step. So tuck the sheet well in between risers and treads, using drawing pins if necessary.

Attic rooms

In positions exposed to harsh winds, a house will tend to rock a little; and the higher you go the more pronounced

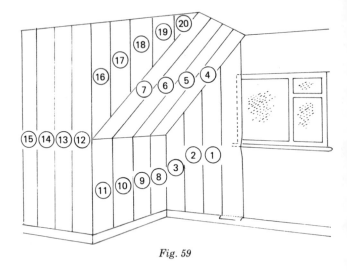

Fig. 59

the rock will be – like a modified upside-down version of the pendulum of a grandfather clock.

This will lead to wider cracks in walls and ceilings than in a ground floor room, which will need careful raking out and stopping up with one of the stoppers on the market that will 'give' with further structural movement. The use of embossed paper is indicated here, as the embossing will slightly flatten out to take up further movement without cracking. Or you can hang a lining paper and emulsion paint over that.

These top rooms will often have a dormer window to take advantage of every inch of room space. There'll be a sloping roof too, which will present difficulties in matching. So, for preference, choose a paper with an indiscriminate pattern.

Procedure for working will vary according to shape and will need careful thinking out in advance. A typical room corner is shown in Fig. 59.

Don't forget to plumb every corner; and never attempt to complete one length over horizontal ceiling, sloping ceiling and perpendicular wall; or the angle between the three is bound to be somewhat out-of-line and you'll be faced with unsightly overlaps and gaps.

Paper the ceiling first (unless you're using emulsion paint on it); then deal with walls and sloping parts – each with separate drops of paper.

Turn exterior corners with the customary 50 mm (2 in.) and interior corners with half or less that amount. At these points, cut the paper longitudinally, hang and join up with the off-cut, as is described on pages 105 and 106. What you do with the horizontal joins between sloping ceiling and perpendicular wall will be determined by the planning of the room, though about 10 to 15 mm ($\frac{3}{8}$ to $\frac{1}{2}$ in.) overlap would be a safe bet.

Enriched corners

In many houses built in the last century when labour was underpaid and man-hours weren't all that important, the external corners of an entrance hall were often rounded to prevent edges from becoming chipped. These rounded corners would be embellished with concave 'dips' at top and bottom, the convex portions in between being indented at each side as is shown in a typical example, Fig. 60. Such enrichments serve a very useful purpose. Furthermore, they look elegant.

Cut the last length of paper before reaching the enrichment, longitudinally to come level with the vertical edge of the enrichment. Trim the off-cut of paper to the width of the enrichment as it turns the right-angled part of the wall immediately above (a).

Hang this, slit and overlap the slits into the concave part of the enrichment.

Carry on with the remainder of the off-cut to match up with the first piece.

Finally cover the enrichment with a narrow strip of paper trimmed exactly to the shape of the concave portion, to match the patterns on both sides and hide any gaps (b).

However carefully you carry out this procedure there's almost bound to be a mismatch somewhere near top and

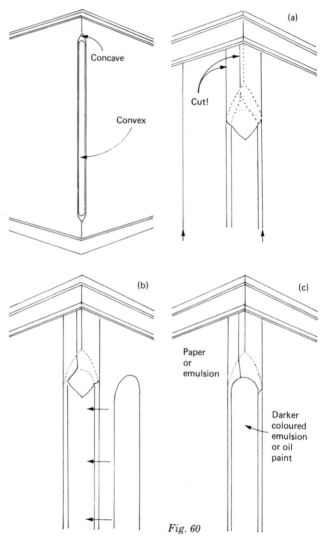

Concave

Convex

(a)

Cut!

(b)

(c)

Paper
or
emulsion

Darker
coloured
emulsion
or oil
paint

Fig. 60

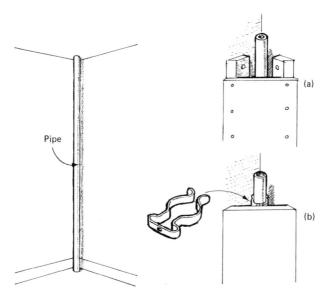

Fig. 61

bottom; and, for this reason it's often better to emulsion paint the whole of the enrichment and bring the paper up to its edges, trimming off neatly (c).

With a spacious house, the walls could be in a deepish red paper and the enrichment in gold paint. A small house would need something considerably lighter in shade, say magnolia, with brown or blue enrichment.

Water and gas pipes

Pipes buried in plaster often lead to cracks showing in the plaster caused by pipe tremble.

If this happens, rake out to expose the pipe, scrape off any rust that may have formed and coat with an anti-rustant. Then give two full coats of bituminous paint and, while still wet, bind round the pipe with a cloth bandage which will act as a cushion. Add more staples for greater security. Replaster the gap.

Where pipes aren't buried but exposed, don't attempt to paper over them. It will only crack at the edges and look shabby. So scrape off rust and touch in with anti-rustant, afterwards painting with a colour similar to that of the wallpaper. Treatment for lead pipes is given on page 40.

You can hide the pipes with 3.2 mm ($\frac{1}{8}$ in.) hardboard pinned to chamfered battens nailed to the wall with masonry nails (Fig. 61a), or make a movable covering with thin wood onto which bulldog clips are fastened at the back. Chamfer the sides of the wood to an angle of 45° to make a snug fit. The clips can then be 'sprung' over the pipe and taken off at will. With this method you cannot, of course, paper over the covering. It will have to be papered or painted separately (Fig. 61b).

No hard and fast rule can be given for pipes that run along the centre of a wall, as is so often the case with old houses. You'll have to use ingenuity here.

Indeed, all painting and decorating calls for ingenuity. You have to think and concentrate. In vulgar words 'Use your loaf!'

14 Common painting faults

Painting suffers from the same annoying disability as gardening. Follow instructions to the letter – or think you have – and things can still go wrong. Here are the most common faults dealt with only summarily in the foregoing text: (numbers in *Prevention for future* refer to those in *Causes*).

Blooming *Symptom*: Varnish turning white on the surface. *Causes*: (1) Painting in damp weather, condensation forming before coatings are dry. (2) Moisture on brushes. *Cure*: Rub gently with equal parts of linseed oil and lemon juice or with 2 parts of olive oil and 1 of vinegar, afterwards polishing with a chamois leather. If obstinate, sand down and recoat. *Prevention for future*: (1) Avoid rainy weather and draughts. (2) Increase ventilation when working and see that brushes are thoroughly dry.

Cissing *Symptoms*: Depressions or small holes in the paintfilm soon after application. *Causes*: (1) Painting over a previously varnished surface without first sanding down. (2) Neglecting to sand down an undercoating that has been on too long before finishing coat is applied (with an alkyd resin paint no sanding is required provided the finish is applied within about a week after undercoating). (3) Minute grease splashes from a cooking stove. *Cure*: Clean, sand down and repaint. *Prevention for future*: (1) Ideally, old varnish should be stripped with a non-caustic paint remover. Reducing existing gloss with a fine well-wetted waterproof abrasive paper and wiping off sludge will be almost as effective, though the new paintfilm will be more prone to damage by knocks and kicks. (2) Gloss paints based on alkyd resin dry first through evaporation of the solvents and later by oxidation. During the evaporation period and after 8 to 10 hours, a new coat will amalgamate with the undercoat. If left much longer than a week it will lie on the surface which will need sanding. (3) Wash down thoroughly and remove all traces of whatever soapless detergent you may use.

Flotation *Symptom*: Streaks of colour different from that of the paint being applied. *Cause*: Mixing different coloured paints from the same manufacturer may cause this trouble if the pigment in, say, a yellow paint is lighter in weight than a blue which you have mixed together to make a green; the yellow pigment can float to the surface in streaks or patches. *Cure*: Sand down lightly and recoat with a green formulated by the manufacturer. *Prevention for future*: Be wary of mixing two paints to achieve a colour not on the manufacturer's shade card. Use the tinting or colour-mixing service provided by the best paint shops.

Grinning (or lack of opacity) *Symptom*: Underlying dark colour showing through a newly applied light-coloured paint. *Cause*: Refracted rays of light reaching the original colour before they can be reflected to the surface. *Cure*: Apply more coats of light colour to ensure adequate film thickness. *Prevention for future*: a more certain alternative to applying more coats is to strip off the original dark paint.

Pattern staining *Symptom*: Light stripes about 50 mm (2 in.) wide and some 400 mm (16 in.) apart on ceilings. *Cause*: Plaster between ceiling joists is cooler than wood and attracts more condensation which, in turn, attracts dust. *Cure*: Wash frequently. *Prevention for future*: If persistent, remove floor boards in room above and insert insulating material between joists.

Reverse pattern staining Dark stripes and larger light patches can occur when relatively cool steel joists are used.

Sheeriness *Symptom*: Dull and glossy patches alternating. *Causes*: (1) Sulphur-laden atmosphere in industrial areas, particularly when lead-based paints are used (rare these days owing to their toxicity). (2) Use of poor quality paints. (3) Thinning down paints during the coating of one area. (4) Differing angles of light reflection. (5) Painting over a surface that is not homogeneous (often occurs when a hole in plaster has been patched). *Cure*: Sand down lightly, adding more coats of a lead-free paint. *Prevention for future*: (1) Don't use lead-based paints, particularly on greenhouses where sulphur sprays may be employed. Any product containing an excess of lead has to state this on the can label. (2) Use only the best quality paints. (3) If a paint kettle is used there should be no need to thin down paint unless directed by the manufacturer. In any case, never carry out thinning during the painting of one surface. Wait until you reach the corner of a room; then the difference won't be noticed. (4) Always lay off in one direction only; then light will be reflected evenly. (5) Try to ensure that any stopping-up of holes is done with a stopper of the same consistency as that of the surrounding surface.

Slow drying *Symptom*: Failure of an emulsion or water paint to become touch-dry in three or four hours and oil paint in, say, 10 hours. *Causes*: (1) Painting in cold, damp or foggy weather. (2) Pressure of grease on the unpainted surface. (3) Use of unsuitable thinners (such as paraffin). (4) Using brushes previously cleaned in paraffin and not washed out properly afterwards. *Cure*: Have a little more patience for paint to dry. If it doesn't after a week, strip, prepare the surface more thoroughly, use only clean brushes and choose your weather. *Prevention for future*: (1) Choose a dry day for working. (2) Clean off all traces of grease, particularly in a kitchen. (3) If thinning is *really* necessary, use turpentine substitute for oil paint, clean water for emulsion and water paint, and cellulose thinner for cellulose paint. (4) Wash brushes in turps substitute.

Spottiness *Symptom*: Brown, grey or black specks appearing on painted walls and ceilings. *Causes*: (1) Mould, diagnosed by the spots increasing in size until they join up with one another. (2) Crystalline residue around gas stoves expelled by minute explosions during cooking. (3) Particles of metal flying from scouring pads round a kitchen sink. (4) Particles of metal from plumbing work. (5) Nail heads rusting when used to secure plasterboard on walls and ceilings. (6) Reverse pattern staining (see above) on cold exposed nail heads. *Cure*: (1) Rub off stains with water and an abrasive cleaning powder and give two applications of a fungicide (from paintshops). Then redecorate. (2) Wipe off with abrasive cleaning powder. (3 and 4) These specks will have rusted; after wiping them off touch in with aluminium primer sealer. (5) Remove rust with emery paper and touch in with zinc chromate primer or aluminium primer sealer before covering with paint. If on wood, punch nail heads well in and stop up depressions with putty or cellulose filler, knifed level. (6) Result of cold steel nail heads attracting dust. Wash off and touch in with paint. *Prevention for future*: (1) Paint that includes a mould-inhibiting agent will function for a time, though the agent tends to leach out in a year or two. (2 and 3) Surround stove and sink with metal or hardboard decorated sheeting. These present a hard surface onto which metal particles won't stick so easily. (4) Temporarily mask out the wall immediately behind plumbing work with a dust sheet. (5) Use non-ferrous nails in future. (6) Punch in nail heads wherever possible, and stop up depressions.

Varnish failure after application *Symptom*: Sticky surface that persists. *Causes*: (1) Recent installation of central heating. (2) Washing with too strong an alkali solution. (3) Use of water-based PVA emulsion polish containing a plasticiser. (4) Use of an aerosol cleaner or polish where the propellent *could* cause trouble. (5) Use of wax polish containing too high a proportion of turpentine. *Cure*: Try washing with turpentine substitute or ammonia solution. If stickiness doesn't respond, strip with a non-caustic paint remover and revarnish. *Prevention for future*: (1) Work when room has reached the warmth of the central heating. (2) Use only a weak detergent solution and wash off immediately. (3, 4 and 5) Don't use polish. Varnish doesn't need it.